Contents

CW01499393

Chinese Wushu Series

Basics of Long-Style Boxing

Cheng Huikun

FOREIGN LANGUAGES PRESS   BEIJING

First Edition   1996

Second Printing   2003

Home Page:
http://www.flp.com.cn
E-mail Addresses:
info@flp.com.cn
sales@flp.com.cn

ISBN 7-119-01538-9
©Foreign Languages Press, Beijing, China, 1996
Published by Foreign Languages Press
24 Baiwanzhuang Road, Beijing 100037, China
Printed by Beijing Foreign Languages Printing House
19 Chegongzhuang Xilu, Beijing 100044, China
Distributed by China International Book Trading Corporation
35 Chegongzhuang Xilu, Beijing 100044, China
P.O. Box 399, Beijing, China
Printed in the People's Republic of China

Chapter One
General Description and Basic Technical Features

Long-style boxing (*Chang Quan*) was, formerly, the general term for *Cha Quan, Hua Quan* and *Hong Quan* boxing styles.

Cha Quan is characterized by alternate movements of opening and closing and clear rises and falls. It stresses leg techniques and wrestling with simple and clear rhythms. Coordination of mind and body movements, plus integration of internal and external exercises, are the two essential points of this boxing style. *Hua Quan* calls for strict execution of movements, mainly of body and mind, clear lines and a strong physique. The moving exercises must be fast; the still exercises should be solid. All movements must be connected in continuity. *Hong Quan* is known for simple movements, strict composition, close attack and defence, and equal stress on hardness and softness.

Long-style boxing or *Chang Quan* is a new style of Chinese boxing developed after the founding of the People's Republic of China. It has exerted tremendous influence on the Wushu sport and enjoys tremendous popularity among the masses. The modern style of *Chang Quan* combines the good points of the *Cha, Hua* and *Hong* boxing styles. It has standardized their hand forms, hand techniques, stances, footwork, leg techniques, balance and jumping movements and, on the basis of the rules for body movements, woven them into different routines, including: scurrying, leaping, jumping, dodging, rising, falling, turning and bending. All movements are flexible, quick, powerful, fully extended in posture, and clear in rhythm. *Chang Quan* is one of the compulsory events in the national Wushu competition and demonstration, as well as in international Wushu competition. The *Chang Quan* known in modern Wushu refers to the newly-composed style of *Chang Quan.*

Chang Quang is complicated in composition. Its movements are executed within a wide range, requiring tremendous physical exertion and quick speed. Constant practice helps to improve the functions of the central nervous system, the cardiovascular system and the respiratory system. It also improves the pliability and elasticity of the muscles and ligaments and flexibility of the joints. It can promote the physical development of children and young people and assist their determination in overcoming difficulties. This is why *Chang Quan* has become a popular sport among children and young people.

Every school of Chinese boxing has its own basic techniques and its own particular style and characteristics. The elements of *Chang Quan* include composition, arrangement, basic movements and difficult movements. Technically speaking, when a man or woman practices *Chang Quan*, he or she must do it with the correct posture and according to clear forms. The practitioner must apply power smoothly, change body movements frequently, follow the hand movements closely with the eyes, breathe naturally, concentrate the mind, and perform the exercises with smooth rhythm; all these aspects are interrelated.

1. Correct Posture

Generally speaking, correct posture refers to the fixed form of the body when the practitioner is in a still position. This is true in the Hook Hand with a Snap Palm and Empty Step as an example. Certain movements also call for relative stillness in a very short time; this is known in Chinese Wushu as "stillness in movement." This can be seen in the Jumping Front Kick.

The basic requirements for correct body posture: keep the head upright, the neck straight, the shoulders low, the chest out, the waist straight (or dropped) and buttocks pulled in. Upper limbs must be fully extended and straight. For example, when you pracitse the Flash Palm (Fig. 2-104), you should drop your shoulders, slightly bend your elbows to make your arms round and place your palm obliquely above your head. The outlines of the lower limbs must be very clear. In practising the Bow Step (Fig. 2-43), the front leg should be bent and the rear leg completely straight. The height of the legs should be suitable for the position of the feet. The posture of the whole body movement should be well-balanced. The implications of attack and defence should be shown both in the external forms and in your mental state when you practise a fixed form of Wushu.

2. Clear Forms

Forms refer to the methods of movements in kicking, striking, throwing, catching and other exercises. The starting and finishing lines, plus the force points should be clear so as to show the technical features of attack and defence in the exercises. For example, when you kick with the heel, the toes should be upward while the sole is forward, with the force point on the heel. In the snap kick, the toes should be forward, the instep flat and the force point on the toes. In the side sole kick, the toes should be turned, the foot sole forward and the force point on the sole. Only in this way can the different hand and leg techniques be differentiated from each other. If you do not strictly follow the rules for the different forms, you cannot express the true significance of their differences; as a result, implications of all attack and defence skills in *Chang Quan* are lost. This is why, in practising *Chang Quan*, you must understand the specific contents and methods of movements for attack and defence skills. You must clearly remember their different lines, locations and force points, and make yourself familiar with the different degrees of applying power and the different speeds of movement.

3. Smooth Power Application

The word "power" refers to the power applied when you do exercises. The power must be either hard or soft. The power should be applied smoothly, yet with an explosive force. If the power is not properly applied, the movements will be stiff and rigid. In *Chang Quan*, you must avoid stiff movements with hard power only. In pushing, chopping, hammering, kicking and elbowing, you should use the power that is first soft and then hard, with the power smoothly applied to the force points. For example, in thrusting your fist in a bow step, you should transmit the power generated from your feet, knees and hips to the thrusting fist through the waist, back and then to the shoulders and elbows. This will ensure that the power from the lower and upper body becomes one. The problem of stiff and rigid movements is not caused by how much power is applied, but by whether it is smoothly applied. Therefore, in practising *Chang Quan*, the power applied should be hard but not stiff, soft but not loose. The degree of hardness and softness should be properly controlled. Moreover, you should use your consciousness to control the application of the power, and coordinate your breathing with the application of power so as to achieve the integration of the external and internal.

4. Varying Body Techniques

Body techniques refer to the various techniques of attack and defence, mainly using the body. The body techniques in the *Chang Quan* routines include "dodging, extending, lying prostrate, lying on the back, turning, recoiling, pushing and leaning against." These body techniques are used with the waist as axis. They are combined with various hand and leg techniques to demonstrate a variety of movements. On the one hand, the body techniques should change from time to time; on the other, the pliability of the chest and waist should be strengthened, so that movements are executed both softly and vigorously. When the movement is soft, it is flexible; when it is hard, it is powerful. Therefore, the body techniques are not isolated movements of the upper part of the body, but closely related with attack and defence implications of the whole exercise and movements of the entire body. If the body techniques are to be used correctly, it is necessary to understand the essential technical points as well as the implications of attack and defence movements. You must know how to use the waist properly to change from one movement to another, and different methods for different movements.

5. Follow Movements Closely

The methods of coordination between the eyes and the movements are called eye techniques. The eye techniques are an important link in the expression of the spirit. Two boxing proverbs say:"Follow the hand movements closely with the eyes," and "The eyes go to where the hands are." In practising boxing, if eye expression is not properly used, the movements have no life and the routine becomes only a rigid set of movements. But if eye expression is coordinated properly with the movements, the inherent spirit and consciousness will be fully expressed through the eyes. The result will be an entire exercise that is well-coordinated and full of life. The methods of coordiantion between the eyes and the movements vary: there are fixed looks and moving looks. A fixed look means fixing your eyes on a certain target; a moving look means moving your eyes along with the movement of a certain part of your body until the movement is finished. Take the Swing Palms with Cross Step in the basic routine as an example. The eyes follow the hands closely to coordinate the whole exercise. The eyes technique is not only closely related with the hand techniques, but also with the movement of the neck. When the fist is thrust forward to the right, if the neck does not move and the head is not turned to the right, you have to look at your hands sideways. Therefore, in the eye techniques, when you move your eyes to the left or right, up or down, the neck and the head have to be turned quickly.

The coordination between the eyes and the movement must be based on the correct execution of the movement. If not correctly executed, it will affect the display of the inherent spirit and consciousness; if not correctly coordinated, it will also affect the quality of the movement. "Similarity in form" is the basis for the "vivid expression of the mind" which, itself, is the highest manifestation of "similarity in form." Neither should be neglected, or the vivid expression of the mind is impossible.

In the use of the eye techniques, you should avoid confusion; i.e., if movement of the eyes is not done properly, the mind will not concentrate. The point is that you should be calm and flexible.

6. Breathe Properly

Because composition of the routines is complicated and the movements are fast, with tremendous physical power required in the *Chang Quan* exercises, there is great need for oxygen. Therefore, proper breathing is very important to achieving the technical level and the longevity of the power. *Chang Quan* stresses abdominal breathing method which result in breathing in order to conserve energy. Only in this way, can the exercise be lasting and balanced.

There are four breathing methods, "lifting," "propping." "accumulating" and "sinking," in the *Chang Quan* routine exercise. The "lifting" method means deep breathing. The abdomen should be held in so as to give the whole body a feeling of lightness and rising. The "propping" method means slow breathing. The whole body should be fully relaxed. The "accumulating" method means short breathing. It should permeate the whole body for the convenience of power application. The "sinking" method requires the practitioner to keep his abdomen solid and make his breath short and even. In jumping and in moving from a lower level to a higher level, the practitioner should use the "lifting" method. In doing still exercises at a higher or lower level, he should use the "propping" method. In making hard and clean fast movements, he should change to the "accumulating" method. When passing from a high level to a lower level, he should use the "sinking" method. When the breathing methods change with the movements, he should never depart from the basic requirement of "conserving the breath." The skillful use of different methods for different exercises in different situations is a matter of importance in the *Chang Quan* routine exercise.

7. Concentration

Concentration training is one of the basic components of Wushu. *Chang Quan* exercises first of all call for concentration of the mind. You should cultivate your awareness of attack and defence skills and display bravery, alertness and fearlessness. Your facial expression should be natural.

You should display this inherent mental state not only in the attack and defence movements, but also in all other movements, not only in the facial expressions, but in the whole set of exercises.

8. Clear Rhythms

In *Chang Quan*, it is also very important to handle the rhythms of the movements, stillness, quickness and slowness. The traditional way is to simulate natural sights and animals in the rhythms, summed up in twelve forms; "move like waves, keep still as a mountain, rise like an ape, fall like a magpie, stand on one leg like a cock, stand on both legs like a pine tree, turn like a wheel, bend like a bow, be light as a leaf, be heavy as iron, move fast like the wind, and move slowly as a soaring eagle." These metaphors vividly reflect the rhythms of the *Chang Quan* exercises.

In doing your exercises, you should move like waves upon waves, in clear rhythms, similar to the feeling of stability and clarity in a situation when thousands of horses are galloping. This is what we call "rhythms in moving" and "stillness in moving." When you are in a state of "stillness," you should stand as firm and powerful as a tall mountain, as if there is nothing powerful enough in the world that can move it.

In leaping, you should do it as cleverly, agilely and

quickly as a monkey. When falling, you must touch the ground as lightly and firmly as a magpie perches on a tree twig.

When you stand on one leg, especially when you change a moving exercise to a still standing exercise, you should perform like a cock when it hears something while walking and stops abruptly with one leg held off the ground; it shows stability of the movement. Standing on both legs, you should be as strong, powerful and firm as a pine tree. There should be a sense of movement when you stand still; i.e., "movement in stillness." Stillness must be closely related with movement.

In turning, you should move your body like a wheel around an axle, and be good at creating an axle centre for your movement, so that the body turns in a round circle. Bending movements include twisting, turning and bending the body. It requires the practitioner to do bending exercises like a bow with resilience. The more you bend the more resilient you become. For example, when you bend your body the either side, it is good if your waist is soft enough to be bent low; but if there is no power generated from the bending movement to enable you to do the immediate movements that follow, you will not be able to continue your exercises coherently. In doing the bending exercises, you should be resilient so as to demonstrate the changes in the movements.

"Light" movements must be made as light as a leaf as if your movements are floating in the air. Heavy movements like hammering and foot stamping must be as heavy and powerful as steel ingots, but there must be no sign of relentlessness in making heavy movements.

Quick movements must be made like a swift and strong gust of wind, but impetuosity should be avoided. If you are impetuous in making movements, the movements will not be accurate, clean, neat and natural. A slow movement should look like an eagle circling slowly in the air. It is slow but not loose. There should be concentration. If the rhythms of a routine are not well handled, the movements will look dull and uninteresting. If there are no "light" movements in a routine, it is difficult to tell which movements are "heavy" ones. If there are no soft movements, there will be no powerful movements. If there is no slow start, it is not possible to show the acceleration. If you cannot stop firmly and steadily, you cannot show your fast movements. The opposites of these contradictions exist in comparison. The more these contradictions are displayed in the movements, the stronger the rhythms.

There are also rhythms in a single exercise. Take the Thread Palm with Crouch Step (Figs. 2-136, 137, 138) for an example. When the practitioner falls suddenly, the speed changes from slowness to quickness. The body movements also change from time to time, sometimes powerful, sometimes soft; and sometimes open, sometimes drawn in. Only when the changes are clear, will people find the exercises interesting, attractive and lively.

The eight aspects described above are interrelated and closely coordinated. They constitute the basic elements of the routine skills of *Chang Quan*. They must all be mastered; only by so doing can you play *Chang Quan* with great proficiency.

Chapter Two
Basic Skills and Basic Movements

The basic skills and basic movements involved in *Chang Quan* include exercises for the shoulders, arms, waist, legs, hands and feet, as well as leaps and balances. In the course of practice, you can do some connecting combinations for bare-handed movements.

The basic skills and basic movements are closely related. Practice of basic skills and basic movements helps to train all parts of the body and quickly build up the special physical qualities for the Wushu sport. This lays a good foundation for learning the routines of different schools of Chinese boxing, both bare-handed exercises and exercises with weapons, as well as improving the technical level.

Constant practice of basic skills and basic movements helps to strengthen the pliability and flexibility of the joints and ligaments, and improve the controlling ability and elasticity of the muscles. Practice of the turning exercises on the ground or in the air helps improve the quality of the movements and prevent injuries. Only persistent practice yields satisfactory results.

To help you grasp the basic skills and basic movements, I would first of all say a few words on the basic hand forms of *Chang Quan*.

Fist (Fig. 2-1): Keep the four fingers closely together and turn them into a fist. Press the thumb tightly on the second joint of the forefinger and middle finger. Keep the fist tightly closed and flat with a straight wrist.

Palm (Fig. 2-2): Keep the fingers together and straight with the thumb bent at the bottom of the forefinger.

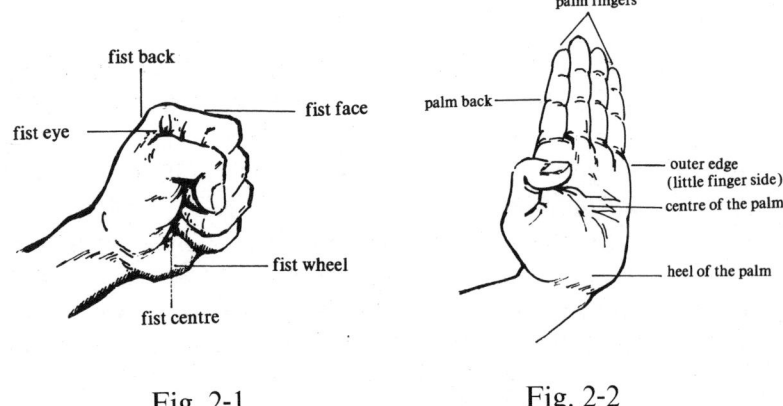

Fig. 2-1

Fig. 2-2

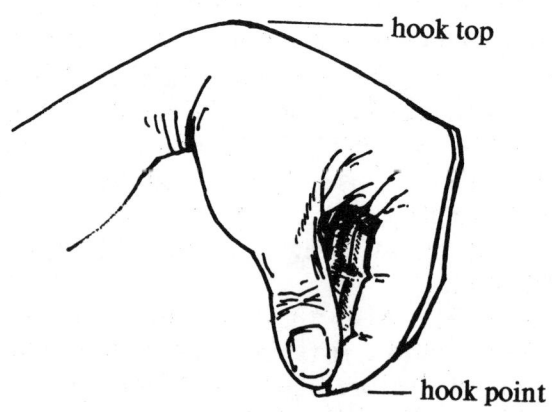

hook top

hook point

Fig. 2-3

Hook (Fig. 2-3): Keep the tips of the thumb and fingers together, and bend the wrist.

1. Shoulder and Arm Exercises

The shoulder and arm exercises are mainly intended to improve the pliability of the ligaments of the shoulder joints and enlarge the range of movement of the shoulder joints. These exercises will increase the power of the arms and improve the nimbleness of the upper limbs and their ability to extend and turn. This will provide the necessary special qualities for learning and mastering different fist and palm techniques. The common methods are shoulder stretch and arm circling.

Shoulder Stretch

Stand facing the stall bars (or an equivalent) a large step away, feet apart with the toes forward to shoulder width. There are three methods:

1. Grasp the bars with both hands, bend the upper part of the body forward (chest out, waist dropped and buttocks in), and keep stretching downward.

2. Ask an assistant to help stretch your shoulders and back rhythmically with both hands (Fig. 2-4).

3. Stand face to face with an assistant, with hands on each other's shoulders, bodies bent forward, and keep stretching each other's shoulders (Fig. 2-5).

Essentials: Keep both arms and legs straight, and shoulders relaxed. The frequency of stretching should increase gradually. Concentrate the stretch points on the shoulders. Auxiliary power should be increased gradually.

You can also stand with your back to the bars, hold the bars with both hands, squat down or lift the body up (Fig. 2-6).

Essentials: Keep the arms straight, shoulders relaxed. Keep the hands as narrowly apart as possible while holding

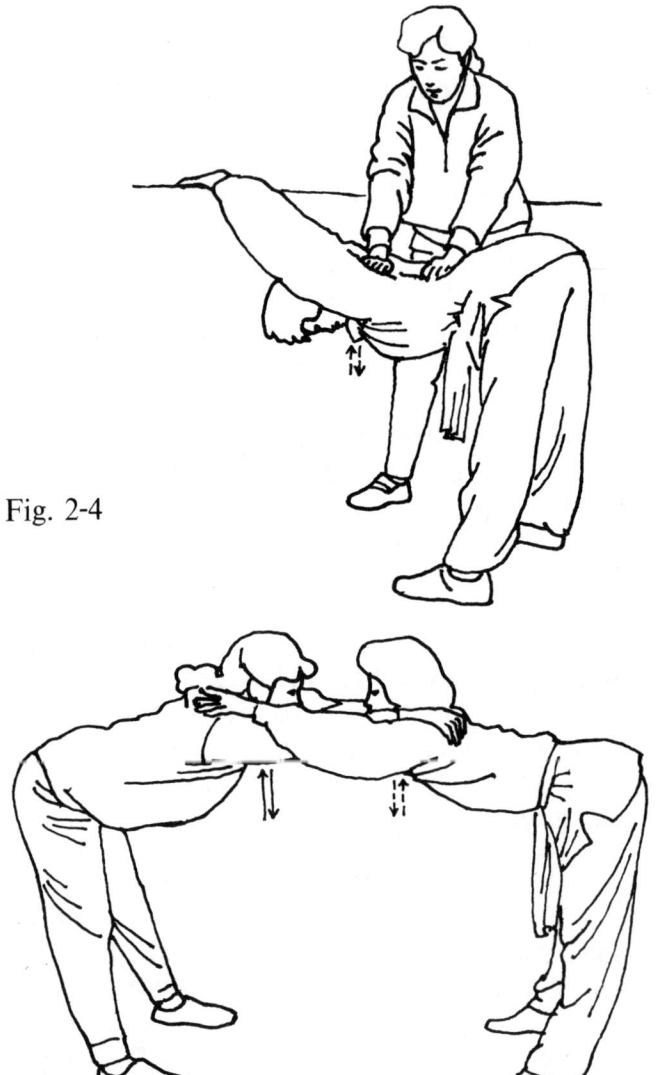

Fig. 2-4

Fig. 2-5

the bars. Downward stretching should be combined with a lifting up motion.

Arm Circling

Stand with feet apart, both arms straight. With the shoulder joints as axles, move the arms round by the side or in front of the body.

1. Move round with one arm. Move the right arm forward, up and backward; this is called backward circling. Move the right arm backward, up and forward; this is called forward circling. Circle with either arm alternately (Fig. 2-7).

2. Move round with both arms. There are mainly three methods:

(1) Circle with both arms moving. Move the left arm from downward to forward, upward and backward for forward circling. Move the right arm from upward to backward, downward and forward for backward circling. Then move the arms in opposite directions (Fig. 2-8). Or move both arms at the same time for forward or backward

Fig. 2-6

circling.

(2) Cross circling. Hold up both arms, and keep them straight. Move the left arm forward, downward and backward, and the right arm backward, downward and forward to draw circles by both sides. Practise with the arms moving alternately.

(3) Circle to the left and right. Move both arms to the right, upward, to the left and downward, to draw circles (Fig. 2-9). Then circle with both arms moving in the opposite direction.

Essentials: Stand with back straight, shoulder joints relaxed and arms straight to draw circles. Use the waist to motivate the shoulders. Look horizontally. The speed of circling should increase gradually.

3. Turn the shoulders. Hold a stick with both hands and move it upward, over the head, backward and return to the original position (Fig. 2-10).

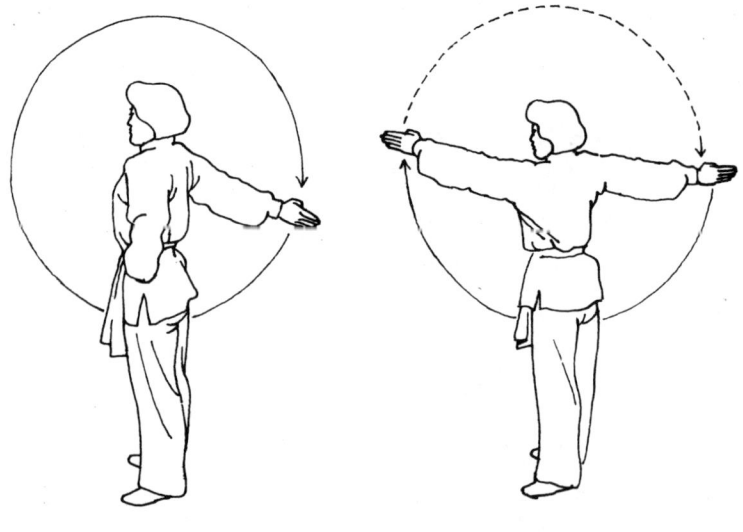

Fig. 2-7   Fig. 2-8

Essentials: Keep both arms straight and gradually narrow the distance between the hands while holding the stick.

2. Leg Exercises

These exercises are mainly intended to improve the pliability, flexibility and muscular power of the legs. They include leg stretch, leg press, legs apart and kick. The exercises should be done by using the legs alternately.

Leg Stretch

This is mainly intended to increase the range of movement of the hip joint, and lengthen the muscles and ligaments of the legs. The exercises include front stretch, side stretch and back stretch.

1. Front leg stretch: Stand with feet together, facing the wall bars or an object of certain height. Raise the left leg

Fig. 2-9   Fig. 2-10

and put the heel on the bar, toes upward, ankle joint bent tightly. Press both hands on the knee or hold the left foot with both hands. Keep the waist straight, hips in and both legs straight. Bend the body forward and downward (Fig. 2-11).

Essentials: Keep both legs straight, left foot flexed, chest out, waist dropped, buttocks in. Gradually increase the angle of stretch and the height of the stretching leg. Improve the pliability of the leg, step by step, by touching the forehead and nose first, and then the lower jaw with the toes (Fig. 2-12).

2. Side leg stretch. Stand on the left leg with one side of the body towards the wall bars, toes slightly outward. Raise the right leg and put the heels on the bar, toes upward, ankle joint bent tightly. Bend the left elbow and raise it upward. Place the right palm on the left side of the chest. Keep both legs straight, waist erect, buttocks out, and bend the body to the right side for stretch (Fig. 2-13).

Essentials: Keep the chest out, extend the hips, and straighten both legs, with right foot flexed. Slowly, step by step, hold the right foot with both hands and rest the upper body on the right leg (Fig. 2-14).

3. Back leg stretch. Stand with feet together, back towards the wall bars, hands on the waist. Stand on the left leg, raise the right leg backward and put the instep on the bar, keeping it flat. Bend the body backward for back stretch (Fig. 2-15). Or bend the body forward and hold an object with both hands so as to increase the height of the back stretch.

Essentials: Straighten both legs and keep flat on the ground the foot of the supporting leg, chest out, buttocks out and waist bent backward.

4. Leg stretch in crouch stance. Stand with feet apart. Squat fully with the left leg bent, with the foot flat on the

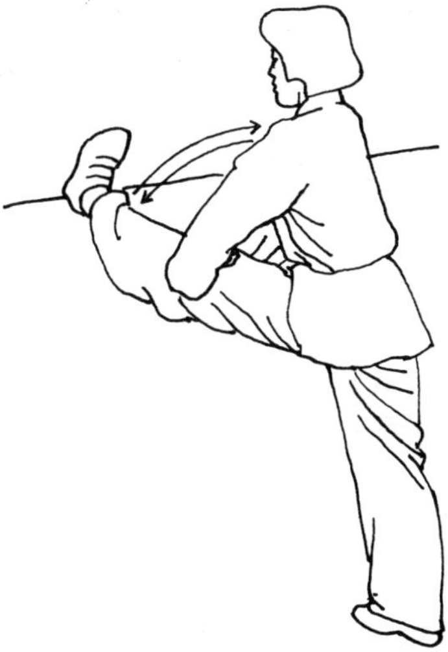

Fig. 2-11 　　　　　　　　Fig. 2-12

Fig. 2-13

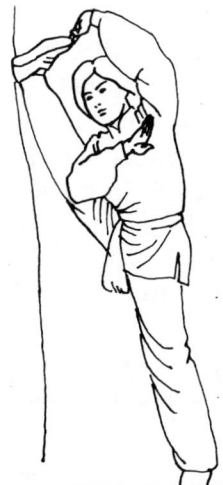

Fig. 2-14

ground. Straighten the right leg, toes inward. Then put the hands separately on the knees or on the outer sides of the feet to form the right crouch stance (Fig. 2-16). Then squat fully with the right leg bent, straighten the left leg, shift the body weight to the right, to form the left crouch stance. During the exercises, the two stances are practised alternately.

Essentials: Keep the chest out and the waist dropped. The shifting of the body weight to either side should not be too fast. Drop the hips so as to keep the buttocks moving as close to the ground as possible.

5. Low leg stretch (or "kiss boots"). Stand with feet apart, one behind the other. Half squat with the back leg bent, front foot flexed. Hold the ball of the foot and pull it forcefully (Fig. 2-17).

Essentials: Except that the supporting leg is in a half squatting position, all movements are the same as in the front leg stretch.

Leg Press

These exercises are intended to increase the pliability of the legs, extend the range of movement of the hip joints and increase the uplifting power of the legs. They include front press, side press and back press. They are done by using the legs alternately.

1. Front leg press. Bend the right leg and raise it, hold the right foot with the left hand, and put the right hand on the knee or on the bars. Then lift the right foot forward and up, knee straight, the outer side of the foot forward (Fig. 2-18). Or stand with your back to an object and ask an assistant to hold the right heel and lift upward (Fig. 2-19).

Essentials: Keep both legs straight, chest out, waist dropped and buttocks in.

2. Side leg press. Bend the right leg and raise it. Hold

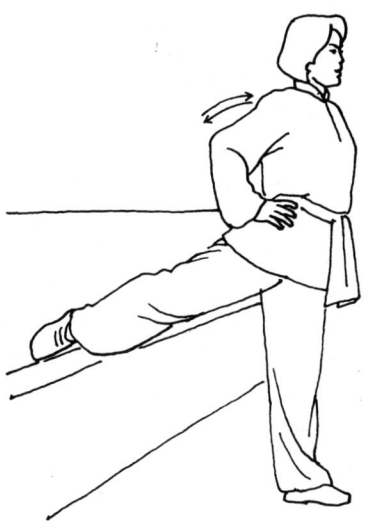

Fig. 2-15

Fig. 2-16

Fig. 2-17

the heel from the inner side of the shank and lift the right leg upward to the right. Raise the left hand above the head with the palm facing upward (Fig. 2-20). If beginners cannot stand firmly on the left leg at the start, they can put their hands on some object for balance. Or ask an assistant to help you execute the side leg press (Fig. 2-21). Essentials: The same as for the Front Leg Press.

3. Back leg press. Place your hands on the bars or on an object for support and stand with feet together. Stand on the left leg, and ask an assistant to lift your right leg upward from behind, knee straight and instep flat. Lean the upper part of the body slightly forward. When your assistant lifts your leg backward and up, you should bend your body backward. This is done in the same way as for the side leg press, but in a different direction. You can also ask your assistant to lift the leg with his or her shoulder. Essentials: The same as for the Back Leg Stretch.

Legs Apart

These exercises are intended to extend the range of movement of the hip joints, and increase the pliability of the legs. They are done together with the leg stretch and leg press exercises. They include the vertical cross and horizontal cross.

1. Vertical cross. Place your hands on the ground or raise hands to shoulder level on both sides (or on the bars). Keep the legs apart to form a vertical line, the back side of the right leg on the ground and foot flexed, with the inner or front side of the left leg on the ground (Fig. 2-22). Use the legs alternately. Essentials: Keep the chest out, waist erect, buttocks dropped and legs straight.

2. Horizontal cross. Place the hands on the ground in front of the body or raise the arms to shoulder level on each side. Keep the legs apart to form a horizontal line,

Fig. 2-18

Fig. 2-19

Fig. 2-20

Fig. 2-21

and the inner side of the feet on the ground (Fig. 2-23).
Essentials: The same as for the vertical cross.
3. Legs apart. A beginner lies on his back on a mat with one leg pressed down (by an assistant on the knee). Raise the other leg upward and ask an assistant to hold the ankle to press the leg downward toward the head (Fig. 2-24). Use the legs alternately.
Essentials: Stay on your back, with the foot of the lifted leg tightly flexed. The assistant should increase the range of movement of the legs gradually, according to the principle of proceeding in an orderly way, and step by step, combining movement with pause. Oblique or sideway lifting is also advisable.

Kick
Kicking is an important part of the leg exercises. It is also one of the principal aspects of training in the basic skills. The kicking exercises are intended to temper the pliability, nimbleness and controlling power of the legs, and can reflect the training quality of the legs. The exercises include straight leg kick and bending leg kick. Use the legs alternately during the exercises.
1. Straight leg kick
(1) Front kick
Stand with feet together, both hands in standing palms or fists, arms raised to the shoulder level on both sides. Move the left foot half a step forward, and stand on the left leg. Kick forcefully towards the forehead with the right flexed foot. Eyes front (Fig. 2-25).
Essentials: Keep the chest out and waist erect. While kicking, lift the leg with a flexed foot and put it down with flat instep, or lift and put down the leg, both with a flexed foot. Draw in both buttocks and the abdomen. Speed up the kick after the foot is above the waist.
(2) Oblique kick

Fig. 2-22

Fig. 2-23

Fig. 2-24

Stand with feet together, both hands in standing palms or fists with arms raised to the shoulder level on the sides. Move the left foot half a step forward, stand on the left leg, and kick forcefully towards the ear of the other side with the right flexed foot. Eyes front (Fig. 2-26).

Essentials: The same as for the front kick. But the oblique kick is started in a different direction.

(3) Side kick

Move the left foot half a step obliquely forward, toes outward, right heel slightly raised. Turn the body slightly to the right, extend the right arm forward and lift the left arm up and backward (Fig. 2-27). Immediately afterwards, keep the right foot flexed and kick towards the right ear. At the same time, bend the left elbow and raise the left hand above the head with the palm facing upward. Bend the right elbow with a standing palm and move it to the front of the right shoulder, or drop it to the crotch. Eyes

Fig. 2-25

Fig. 2-26

front (Fig. 2-28). This is called the left side kick when the left leg is used, or the right side kick when the right leg is used.

Essentials: Turn the body to either side, relax the buttocks, and keep the chest out and waist erect. The raised hand should be swung upward behind the ear on the same side.

(4) Outside kick

The starting position is the same as for the front kick. Move the left foot half a step obliquely forward. Keep the right foot flexed, and kick upward to the left side. Move the right leg in front of the body to the right side and then land it, leg straight, by the left leg. Eyes looking forward. Snap the right palm to the upper right, if you wish (Figs. 2-29, 30).

Essentials: Keep the chest out, waist erect, and the buttocks relaxed and extended. Straighten the legs. The range of movement of the leg should be wide and it should be moved in the shape of a fan.

(5) Inside kick

The starting position is the same as for the front kick. Move the left foot half a step forward to the left. Hook the right foot, toes inward, and kick to the upper right. Then move the right leg in front of the body to the upper left, leg straight, and land it by the outer side of the left foot. Use the left palm to clasp the right sole (with or without a snapping sound) on the upper left. Eyes front (Figs. 2-31, 32).

Essentials: Keep the chest out and waist erect. Relax the buttocks. Keep the legs straight. The range of the inside kick should be large and fan-shaped.

(6) Back kick. Stand with feet together, arms naturally down. Move the left foot half a step forward, ball on the ground. Swing both arms forward. Shift the body weight

Fig. 2-27

Fig. 2-28

Fig. 2-29

Fig. 2-30

backward. Stand on the right leg. Move the left foot backward, leg straight or flexed, and kick backward. Swing both arms upward in front of the body (Fig. 2-33).

Essentials: Keep the chest out, extend the buttocks and lean the body slightly backward. Keep the supporting leg straight, arms naturally straight.

2. Bent leg kicks

(1) Spring kick. Stand with arms akimbo. Bend the left leg and raise it, thigh to the hip level and instep stretched flat (Fig. 2-34). When the knee is raised nearly to the hip level, the movement should be quick and powerful. Kick (spring) the shank forward so as to form a straight line with the thigh. Keep the right leg straight or slightly bent to support the whole body (Fig. 2-35).

Essentials: Keep the chest out, waist erect and buttocks in. The kicking of the shank should be quick and powerful. Keep the instep flat. The bending and stretching movements should be clear and the force points accurate.

(2) Heel kick

It is the same as for the spring kick. The only difference is that the toes should be hooked with the force point on the heel (Fig. 2-36).

Essentials: The same as for the spring kick, but stress should be placed on the hooking of the toes.

(3) Side sole kick

Stand with arms akimbo, move the right foot forward to the left side of the left foot, toes outward, and cross the legs, slightly bent (Fig. 2-37). Stand on the right leg, straighten it, bend the left leg and raise it, keep the left foot inward, and kick with the heel, powerfully, to the upper left, with the power on the heel. Bend the body to the right side. Eyes left front (Fig. 2-38).

Essentials: Keep the knee out, relax the buttocks, kick with the outer side of the foot upward powerfully, with an

Fig. 2-31　　　　　　Fig. 2-32

Fig. 2-33　　　　　　Fig. 2-34

accurate force point.

Sweep

Sweep is a turning leg exercise. There is a forward sweep and backward sweep.

1. Forward sweep

Bend the right leg and move the left foot backward to behind the right foot. Raise the right arm to shoulder level on the right side, bend the left elbow with fingers up and move it in front of the right shoulder. Turn the head to the right, eyes straight ahead (Fig. 2-39). Turn the upper part of the body 180 degrees to the left. At the same time, swing the left arm to the left side of the body, slightly above shoulder level. Swing the right arm naturally to the right side of the body, fingers downward (Fig. 2-40). Continue to turn the upper part of the body to the left, left foot outward. Move the right palm from behind,

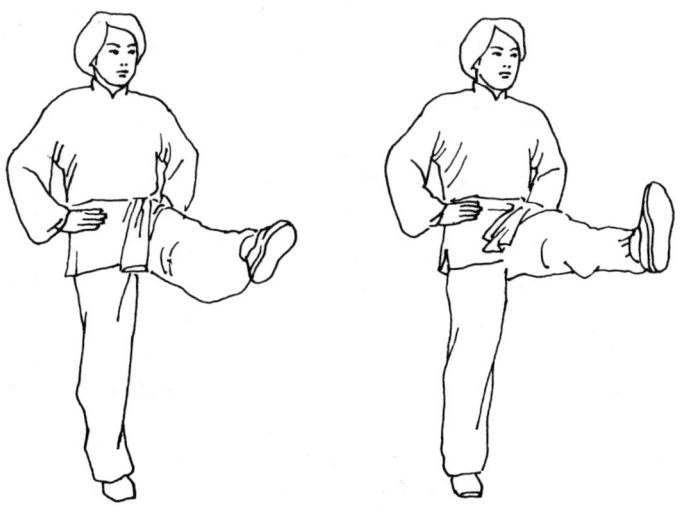

Fig. 2-35   Fig. 2-36

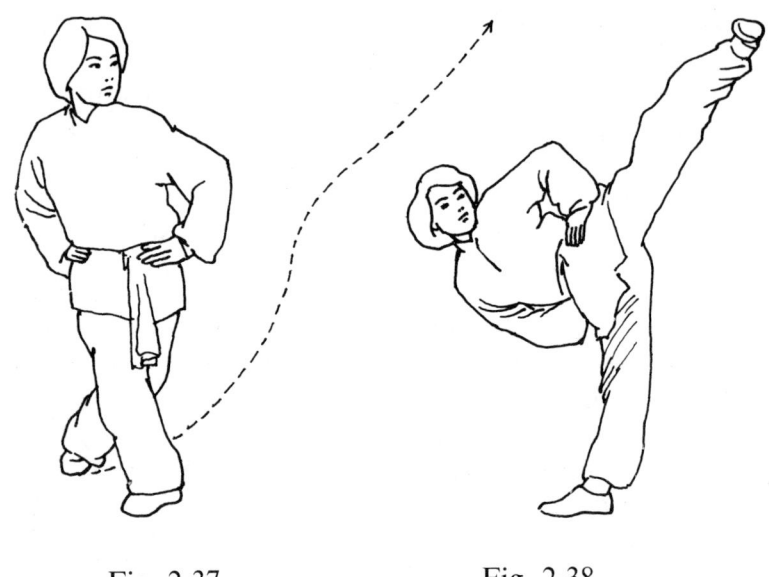

Fig. 2-37   Fig. 2-38

upward and forward in a curve, with elbow bent, in front
of the body. At the same time, bend the left elbow, fingers
up, and move the arm in front of the body, thrusting it
upward above the inner side of the right arm (Fig. 2-41).
Continue to turn the body to the left. Place the left palm
above the head, thumb side down. Immediately drop the
right palm and swing it behind the body, turning it into a
hook hand, fingers up. Bend the left leg with left heel off
the ground. Use the ball of the left foot as axis and
straighten the right leg, toes inward and sole on the
ground. Sweep it forward with a 360-degree turn (Fig.
2-42).

Essentials: Keep the head upright and eyes front while
turning the body, and keep the upper part of the body
erect. In the course of the sweep keep yourself in the right
crouch stance from beginning to end and keep your bal-

Fig. 2-39

Fig. 2-40

Fig. 2-41

Fig. 2-42

ance. Remember to keep the right knee straight and the whole foot on the ground.

2. Backward sweep

Bend the left leg to a half squat and straighten the right leg to form a left bow step. At the same time, push palms forward horizontally from both sides of the waist, fingers up and little finger side forward. Eyes front (Fig. 2-43). Keep the left toes in and bend the left leg to a full squat to form a right crouch stance. At the same time, turn the upper part of the body to the right and lean forward. Put both palms on the ground inside the right leg while turning the body, with the left hand ahead of the right hand. By the inertial power generated from the turning of the body, and with the ball of the left foot as axis, sweep backward with a turn of 360 degrees, right sole on the ground (Figs. 2-44, 45, 46).

Essentials: Turn the body, lean forward, put the hands on the ground and the sweeping movement should be continuous and movements of the upper and lower limbs should be connected.

3. Waist Exercises

The waist is the central part connecting the upper and lower parts of the body. The four elements—hand, eye, body and foot techniques—are affected by the waist in concentrated form. The principal waist exercises include bending forward, bending backward into bridge, bending forward and backward, turning the body with arms sweeping, and turning the waist over.

Bending Forward

Stand with feet together, lock the fingers together and raise the hands up, arms straight and palms up. Bend the upper part of the body forward and keep the hands as close to the ground as possible (Fig. 2-47). With the fingers

Fig. 2-43

Figs. 2-44, 45

Fig. 2-46

apart, hold the heels so as to gradually place the chest close to the legs. Maintain this position for a few minutes before straightening the back (Fig. 2-48). Also turn the body to the left or right, hands on the ground outside the feet.

Essentials: Keep both legs straight, chest out, waist dropped, buttocks in, bending the body forward.

Bending Backward

Stand with feet apart at shoulder width, keep the arms straight and raised. Bend backward, face upward, chest out, hands on the ground, to form a bridge (Fig. 2-49).

A beginner is advised to lie on his or her back, knees and elbows bent, with hands and feet on the ground. Push the hands, press with the feet and thrust the chest out to form a bridge.

Essentials: Keep the waist erect, buttocks out, back straight and heels on the ground.

Bending Forward and Backward

Stand with feet a little more than shoulder width apart, raise the arms and keep bending the body forward and then backward, with waist and hip joints as the axis and arms swinging forward and backward, legs straight. A beginner is advised to use the protective method. An assistant holds his or her back by the waist, standing face to face, and helps him or her do the exercise (Fig. 2-50).

Essentials: The bending movements should be quick with the range of movement gradually increased. The movements should be compact and elastic.

Turning Body

Stand with feet a little more than shoulder width apart, and arms naturally down. Bend the body forward. With the hip joint as axis, stretch the arms forward to the lower left, and turn the upper part of the body around to the front, to the right, backward and to the left (Figs. 2-51,

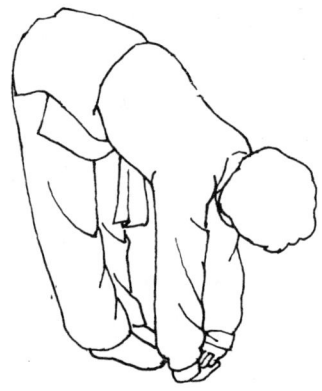

Fig. 2-47

Fig. 2-48

Fig. 2-49

52).

Essentials: Stand firmly with both feet and increase the turning range as much as possible.

Turning Waist Over

Bend the right leg at the knee and move the left leg to behind the right foot, ball on the ground and leg straight, to form a cross step. Raise the right arm to the right shoulder level. Place the left palm up, and swing it to the right shoulder, with fingers up. Eyes to the right forward (Fig. 2-39).

Bend both legs slightly, and move the left arm downward to the left in a semicircle and then to the left side of the body, palm backward. Turn the right arm inward with the palm backward. Bend the body forward. Eyes front (Fig. 2-53).

Move the left palm upward in a circle and the right hand downward in a circle, until the two arms form a straight line. Bend the upper part of the body to the same height. Continue to turn the torso to the upper left and bend backward. Turn both feet with the balls as axis. Place the toes forward, and move both arms, left arm down and right arm up in a circle to both sides of the body. Chest out, face up and eyes looking to the rear (Fig. 2-54).

Continue to turn the upper part of the body, putting the left foot out, legs slightly bent, and moving the right heel to form a cross step. Move the left arm backward and the right arm forward to describe a circle. At the same time turn both forearms outward, with fingers pointing forward and backward, respectively. Eyes right front (Fig. 2-55).

Essentials: Relax both arms and swing them close to the body to form a circle. The turning should be quick.

4. Balance Exercises

Balance is a still movement formed in various stances

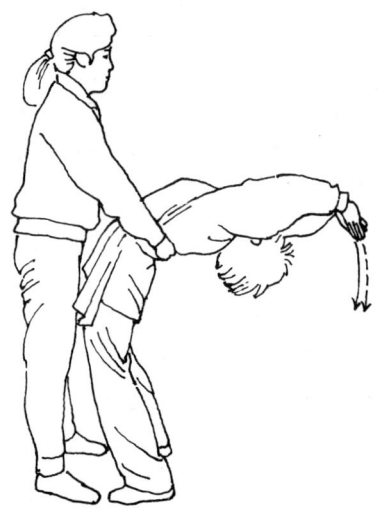

Fig. 2-50

Fig. 2-51   Fig. 2-52

Fig. 2-53   Fig. 2-54

Fig. 2-55

with one leg supporting the body and the other in the air. Balances are divided into lasting balance and unlasting balance. A lasting balance calls for two seconds or more of stillness when the balance movement is completed. An unlasting balance calls for only a moment of stillness when the movement is completed. The completion of the balance movement not only calls for the pliability of the waist and buttocks, but also for good muscle control ability. There are many kinds of balances, but here I will only deal with three.

Raised Knee Balance

Keep the right leg straight to support the body, bend the left leg and raise it (above the waist level) with shank obliquely down. Keep the instep flat and in front of the right leg. Eyes left front (Fig. 2-56).

Essentials: Keep the leg steady and firm, and raise the knee to above the waist level and close to the left chest, with instep in front of the right leg.

Swallow Balance

Stand on the right leg to support the body, bend the left leg at the knee and raise it. Then kick up backward, arms raised on both sides, and lean the upper part of the body forward. Eyes front (Fig. 2-57).

Essentials: Keep the chest out and extend the stomach, with the upper part of the body slightly above hip level, head lifted and eyes front. Keep both legs straight, with the left instep flat and higher than the top of the head to form an arch with the body.

Back Cross-legged Balance

Bend the right leg to a half squat and bend the left knee. Hook the left foot and place it tightly against the back side of the right knee. Turn the hands into upright palms and push them out from both sides (Fig. 2-58).

Fig. 2-56

Fig. 2-57

Fig. 2-58

Essentials: Stand firmly on the right leg with the upper part of the body erect.

5. Hand Form and Hand Technique Exercises

Hand form and hand technique exercises are the basic methods of training the upper limbs, combining the three forms of fist, palm and hook with the movements of thrusting, blocking, pushing and flashing.

Hand Forms
They are described at the beginning of this chapter.

Hand Techniques
1. Thrusting fist (including fist facing down and fist facing sideways)

Stand with feet a shoulder width apart. Hold the fists to both sides of the waist, fingers facing up, and elbows back. Keep the chest out, the stomach in and the waist erect (Fig. 2-59). Thrust the right fist forward forcefully from the waist side, turning the body at waist. Turn the right forearm inward after the elbow joint passes the waist and apply power to the fist, arm straight to shoulder height. At the same time, draw the left elbow backward (Fig. 2-60). Use the hands alternately in practice.

Essentials: Relax the shoulders. The thrusting of the fist should be quick and forceful. Turn the waist and turn the forearm quickly in good coordination with the thrust.

2. Chopping fist (including forward chopping, side chopping and swing chopping).

Stand with feet together, raise the right fist upward, arm straight, and place the left fist to the waist (Fig. 2-61). Chop the right fist straight down quickly, and apply the power to the fist wheel (Fig. 2-62). Chopping downward in a vertical circle by swinging the arm is called swing chopping.

Fig. 2-59

Fig. 2-60

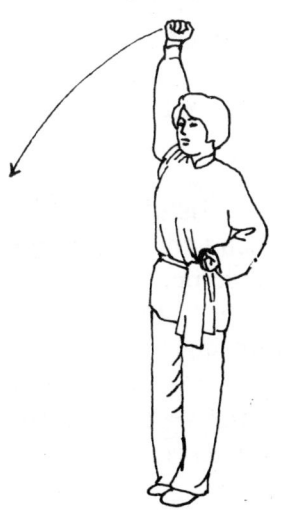

Fig. 2-61

Fig. 2-62

45

Essentials: Chop downward with arm straight—quickly and forcefully.

3. Blocking fist

Stand with feet together, and withdraw the left fist to the waist side. Move the right fist to the left and upward. Move it past the head and to the upper right in a circle. Hold arm straight up. Eyes left front (Fig. 2-63).

Essentials: Relax the shoulders, and turn the forearm inward, elbow slightly bent.

4. Swing-up fist

Stand with feet together, move the left fist to the waist side and swing the right fist backward to a downward angle. Immediately turn the body to the left, move the left foot forward and bend the knee to form a bow step. Move the right fist downward, up forward, arm straight, in an arc to strike. Place fist no higher than the shoulder level, with power applied to the palm. This is called forehand arc fist (Fig. 2-64). Strike backward with arc fist, and apply power to the fist wheel, fist back or fist centre. This is called backhand arc fist.

Essentials: Fist should not be played above the shoulder. Keep the arm straight.

5. Hammer fist

Stand with feet together, raise the right fist up, turn the left forearm outward with palm up, bend the elbow and withdraw the palm to the front of the abdomen (Fig. 2-65). Bend both legs to a half squat, bend the right arm and hammer downward with the fist, and hitting the left palm with the back of the fist (Fig. 2-66).

Essentials: Keep the chest out and the waist low, and hammer the fist close to the body, with power applied to the back of the fist.

6. Sweeping side fist

Stand with feet together, withdraw the left fist to the

Fig. 2-63

Fig. 2-64

Fig. 2-65

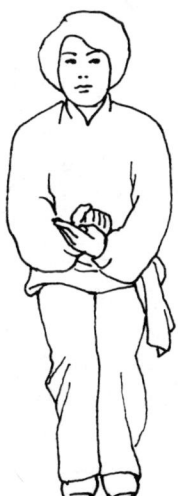

Fig. 2-66

waist side, and swing the right fist downward and obliquely backward (Fig. 2-67). Then swing the right fist obliquely upward to strike in an arc, arm slightly bent (Fig. 2-68).

Essentials: The line of movement of the fist should be curved, with power applied to the fist face, and the arm slightly bent.

7. Pushing palm

Stand with feet together, arms bent at elbow and palms up. Withdraw them to the waist side, turn the left forearm inward and with power on the heel of the palm, push the palm forcefully forward. Turn the waist to the left while pushing, extend the shoulders forward, and straighten the arm to shoulder level. At the same time, draw the right elbow backward (Fig. 2-69). Practise with either palm.

Essentials: Thrust the chest out, keep the abdomen in and waist erect. Relax the shoulders, and push the palm quickly and powerfully. At the same time, the movements of turning the waist, dropping the wrist and turning up the palm should all be done smoothly.

8. Flash palm

Stand with feet together, and place the left palm at the waist side. When the right palm is moved away from the body to the right and upward in an arc above the head, snap the wrist and flash the palm with arm bent in an arc. Keep the palm forward, the tiger's mouth down, with the eyes following the movement of the right palm. When the palm is flashed, turn the head to the left, eyes left front (Figs. 2-70, 71). Use the hands alternately in practice.

Essentials: Snap the wrist, flash the palm and turn the head at the same time.

9. Horizontal palm chop

Stand with feet together, bend the left elbow and put the left palm on the waist. Strike to the left with the right palm up, or strike to the right with the right palm down (Figs.

Fig. 2-67

Fig. 2-68

2-72, 73).

Essentials: Keep the arms straight and apply the power to the outer side of the palm.

10. Press palm downward

Stand on the right leg, bend the left leg at knee and raise it upward. Press the right palm downward in front of the left knee, palm down (Fig. 2-74).

Essentials: Apply power to the palm and keep the arm slightly bent.

11. Thrust palm

Stand with feet together. Press the right palm down in front of the body and thrust the left palm forward from above the back of the right palm. Keep palm up, and arm straight (Fig. 2-75).

Essentials: Keep the palm up. First bend the arm and then extend it to thrust the palm forward, or thrust it forward along a certain part of the body with the power

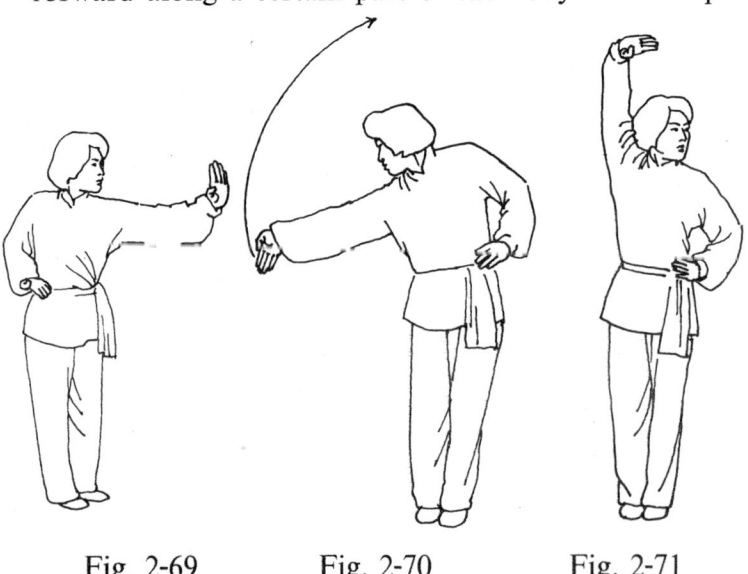

Fig. 2-69   Fig. 2-70   Fig. 2-71

Fig. 2-72

Fig. 2-73

Fig. 2-74

Fig. 2-75

applied to the fingers.

12. Snap palm

Stand with feet together. Bend the left elbow and withdraw it to the waist. Move the right palm from below and swing it forward, arm straight. Snap the wrist to form an upright palm (Figs. 2-76, 77).

Essentials: Relax the wrist and snap it. Apply the power to the fingers.

13. Push elbow

Stand with feet together. Bend the right arm at elbow, clench the fist and raise it horizontally in front of the chest, palm down. Place the left palm against the right fist, eyes left front (Fig. 2-78). Push the right elbow forward or sideward, and press the left palm against the right fist. Eyes right front (Fig. 2-79).

Essentials: Relax the shoulders and arms and apply the power to the elbow.

14. Forearm block

Bend the right arm at elbow, turn the forearm outward and raise it, fist centre outward (Fig. 2-80).

Essentials: Turn the forearm while raising it. Bend the elbow and block above the head, power applied to the forearm.

15. Parry with elbow (inward parry and outward parry)

Bend the left arm at elbow with the hand clenched, keep the forearm erect, or obliquely erect in front of the body. Turn the forearm inward and keep the fist centre towards the inner side of the body. This is called inward parry (Fig. 2-81). Bend the left arm at elbow with the hand clenched, turn the forearm outward and move it to the outer side of the body. This is called outward parry (Fig. 2-82).

Essentials: Pay attention to turning the forearm inward or outward while moving it, and apply power to the forearm.

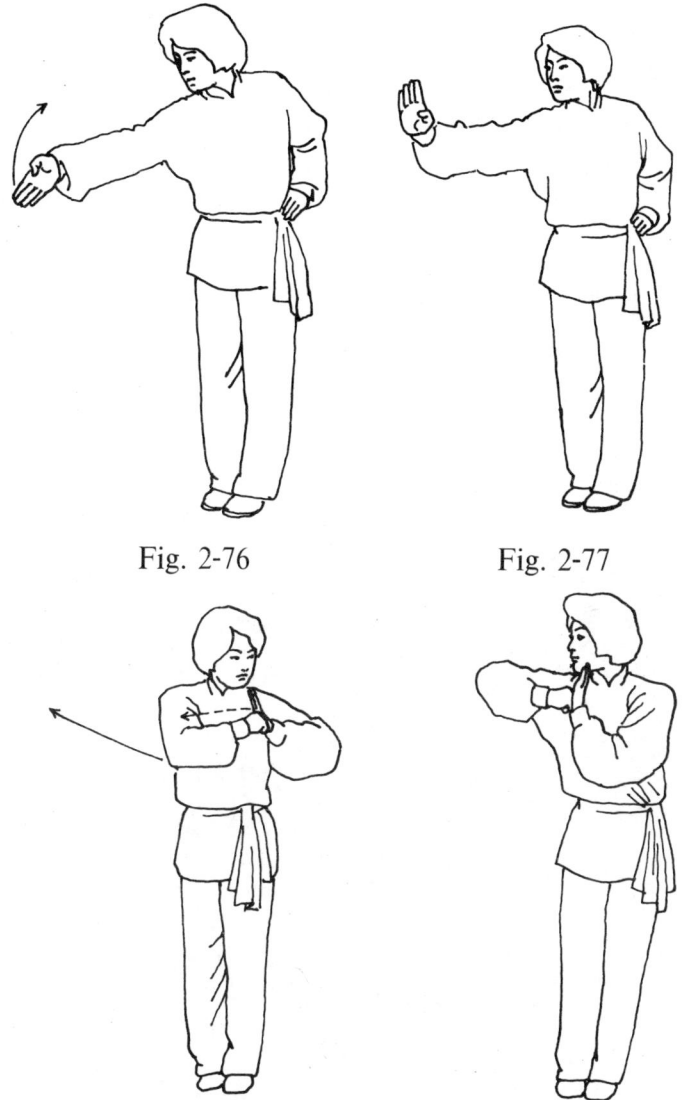

Fig. 2-76

Fig. 2-77

Fig. 2-78

Fig. 2-79

Fig. 2-80   Fig. 2-81

Fig. 2-82

6. Stances and Footwork

Exercises for stances and footwork are intended mainly to increase the speed and power of the legs, in order to improve their nimbleness and stability in the movements.

Stances

Stances refer to still movements of the lower limbs. They are the links connecting the different movements in the whole composition of a routine. Whether the stances are correct or not directly affects the movements and their quality.

1. Bow step

Move the left foot a big step forward (with the length about five times of your foot), with the toes of the foot turned slightly inward. Bend the left leg to a half squat (the thigh nearly level). The knee should form a perpendicular angle with the foot. Straighten the right leg, foot turned inward (obliquely forward), with both feet completely on the ground. Eyes front (Fig. 2-83). It is called the left bow step when the left leg is bowed, and the right bow step when the right leg is bowed.

Essentials: Bend the front leg and straighten the rear leg. Both heels must not be off the ground. Keep the chest out, and drop the waist and buttocks. The toe of the front foot should form a straight line with the heel of the rear foot.

2. Horse-riding step

Keep the feet horizontally apart with the length about three times of your foot, toes forward. Bend the knees to a half squat. Thighs should be nearly level, and both feet on the ground. Keep the body weight between the legs, and put the hands by the waist (Fig. 2-84).

Essentials: Keep the head upright, chest out, waist dropped. The feet should be properly apart and the heels outward.

3. Crouch stance

Stand with feet apart, bend the right leg to a full squat, with thigh on the shank. Keep the right foot fully on the ground, and toes and knee joint outward. Keep the left leg straight, toes turned inward and the whole foot on the ground. Put the hands by the waist. Eyes left front (Fig. 2-85). It is called the left crouch stance when the left leg is crouched, and the right crouch stance when the right leg is crouched.

Essentials: Keep the body upright, chest out, waist and hips dropped and right leg bent to a full squat. The outer side of the left foot should not be off the ground and toes not turned up or outward.

4. Empty step

Stand with feet apart, one behind the other. Turn the right foot 45 degrees outward, bend the leg to a half squat,

Fig. 2-83   Fig. 2-84

left heel off the ground. Keep your instep flat, toes turned slightly inward and lightly on the ground, leg slightly bent, and body weight on the right leg. Eyes front (Fig. 2-86). It is called the left empty step when the left foot is in front, and the right empty step when the right foot is in front.

Essentials: Keep the body upright, chest out and waist dropped.

5. Seated step

Cross the legs to a full squat, left foot turned outward and the whole foot on the ground. Keep the ball of the right foot on the ground, hips sitting on the right shank and close to the heel. Place the hands by the waist. Eyes left front (Fig. 2-87).

Essentials: keep the chest out, waist dropped, and legs tightly against each other. Make the seated step steady and firm.

Footwork

Footwork refers to the varied movements of the lower limbs. There are many kinds of footwork. Described in the following are six:

1. Forward step and backward step

Forward step: move one foot forward.

Backward step: move one foot backward.

The space of the step depends on the requirement of the next movement.

2. Front cross step

Move the right foot one step across the left leg to form the cross step (Fig. 2-88).

Essentials: While making a front cross step, turn the toes outward, waist erect.

3. Kick step

Bend the left leg slightly, hands on the waist (Fig. 2-89). Raise the right foot, and jump forward with the left foot. Kick the left foot with the right foot in the air. Eyes left

Fig. 2-85

Fig. 2-86

Fig. 2-87

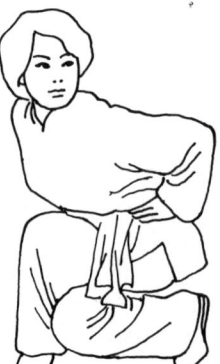

front (Fig. 2-90). Land the right foot first and then the left foot.

Essentials: After jumping into the air, keep the upper part of the body upright and the left side in front. Do not jump too high.

4. Skipping step (Hopping step)

Move the right foot forward, step with the left foot and raise the leg, knee bent. Step with the right foot quickly to jump forward. Land the right foot first, and then land the left foot forward. Eyes front (Figs. 2-91, 92).

5. Back cross step

Bend the left leg to a half squat, move the right foot one step horizontally behind the left foot, and cross the legs to form a back cross step (Fig. 2-93).

Essentials: The same as for the front cross step.

6. S step (Circular walking step)

Stand with hands on waist, elbows bowed outward and legs slightly bent. Change steps obliquely and quickly. The toes of right foot turn outward and the toes of the left foot turn inward, each step slightly bigger than shoulder breadth. Walk along a curved line. Eyes front (Figs. 2-94, 95, 96).

Essentials: Keep the chest out, waist erect, the body in a half squatting posture, and body weight balanced. There should be no rises and falls. Walk from heel to toe and turn the waist.

7. Jumping exercises

The jumping exercises call for movements in the air. They are good for improving the power of the legs and the spring ability. They are part of the exercises for the basic movements. The common basic jumping movements include jumping front kick, jumping and spinning inside kick, flying lotus kick and butterfly.

Fig. 2-88

Fig. 2-89

Fig. 2-90

Fig. 2-91

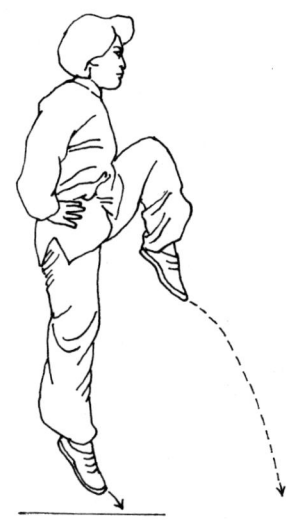

Fig. 2-92

Fig. 2-93

Fig. 2-94

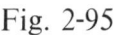

Fig. 2-95

Fig. 2-96

Jumping Front Kick

Stand with the right leg to support the body, bend the left leg at the knee and raise it. Raise the right fist, arm straight. Bend the left arm at the elbow and open the palm in front of the right shoulder. Eyes left front (Fig. 2-97).

Drop the left foot to the left side, toes turned outward, legs slightly bent. Change the right fist to palm and cut downward along the front of the left shoulder, arm straight, fingers forward. Withdraw the left palm to under the right armpit simultaneously with the downward cut, the side of the upper part of the body forward (Fig. 2-98).

Step with the left foot and jump up. Kick the left foot with the right foot in the air. At the same time, move the arms downward and cross them in front of the body. Then swing the left arm forward and right arm backward, both arms straight. Extend the left shoulder forward. Eyes front (Fig. 2-99).

Land the right foot, followed immediately with the left foot stepping forward, and shift the body weight forward (Fig. 2-100).

Move the right foot forward, from heel to toe on the ground, and jump up, body in the air. Kick the left leg forward and upward. Move the arms forward from below and upward to strike the left palm with the back of the right hand over the head (Figs. 2-101, 102).

In the air, move the right leg forward for a upward kick, with instep tightened. Bend the left leg at the knee and tighten the instep. At the same time, drop the right palm to strike the right instep. Swing the left arm to above the side of the body, and bend the upper part of the body slightly forward. Eyes on the right palm (Fig. 2-103).

Essentials: The movement of the kick should be completed at the highest point of the leg in the air. The striking of the instep with the palm should be continuous,

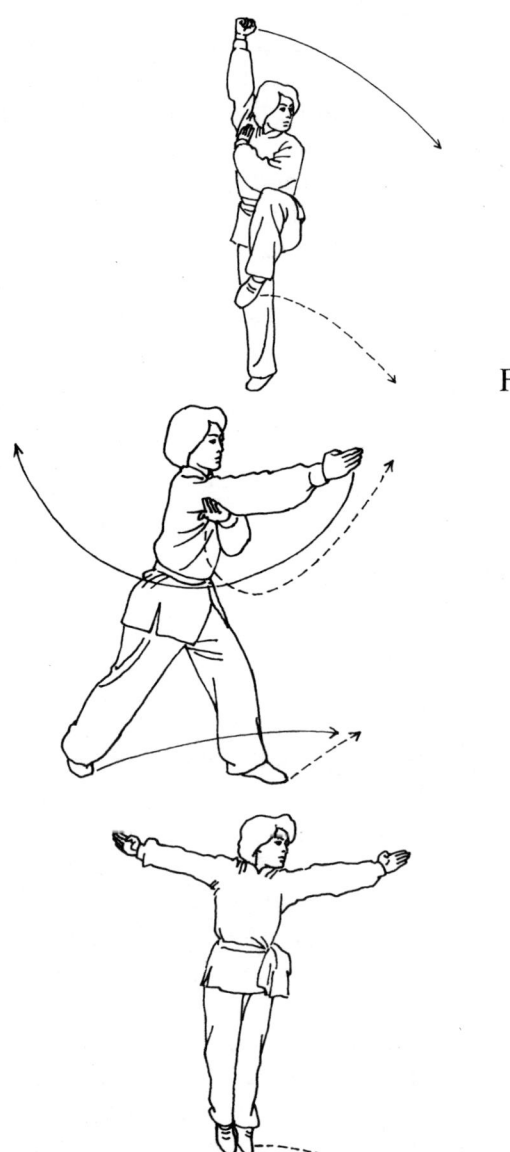

Fig. 2-97

Fig. 2-98

Fig. 2-99

Fig. 2-100

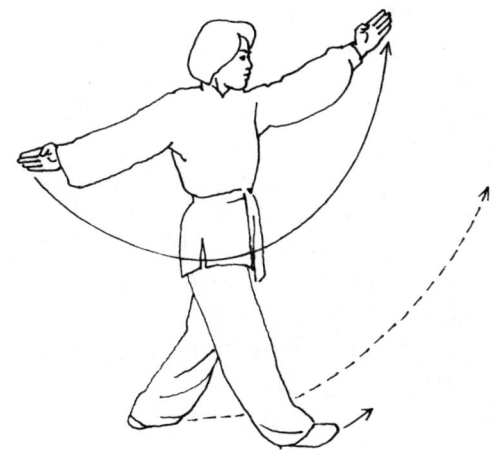

Fig. 2-101

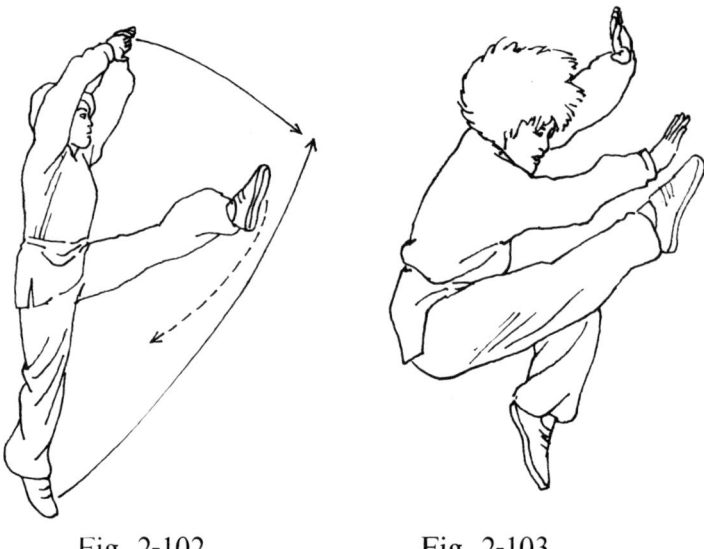

Fig. 2-102   Fig. 2-103

accurate and loud. While in the air, keep the chest out and waist erect, and lean the upper part of the body slightly forward. Don't draw the chest in, nor drop the buttocks.

Jumping and Spinning Inside Kick

Stand on the right leg to support the body, left toes lightly touching the ground. Flash the right palm to the right above the head, and raise the left arm to the shoulder level on the left side (Fig. 2-104).

Move the left foot forward to the left, and move the right foot immediately forward to the left with the ball of the foot on the ground, toes turned inward, legs slightly bent, ready to jump. Move the left arm, elbow bent, to the front of the right shoulder. At the same time, raise the right arm and turn the upper part of the body to the left to bend forward (Fig. 2-105).

Shift the body weight to the right, step with the right foot and jump, raising the left leg and swinging it to the upper left. Turn the upper part of the body to the upper left, at the same time swinging the arms downward and then towards the upper left. Continue to turn the body to the left and swing the right leg upward to execute an inside kick. Strike the right sole with the left hand in front of the body, and keep the left leg naturally down or place it by the left side of the body, knee bent (Figs. 2-106, 107).

Essentials: While executing an inside kick with the right leg, the leg should be straight and close to the body and moved from outside to inside in the shape of a fan. The left leg should be smoothly extended while it is swung outward. Keep the whole body in the air while executing a snap kick. The snapping point should be close to the body. The movements should be well coordinated. The body turn should be no less than 270 degrees.

Flying Lotus Kick

Stand on the right leg to support the body, and raise the

Fig. 2-104   Fig. 2-105

67

Fig. 2-106   Fig. 2-107

left leg, knee bent. Push the right upright palm forward. Extend the shoulders forward and raise the left
arm obliquely behind the body. Eyes front (Fig. 2-108).

Put the left foot forward down, and move the right foot
forward, knees bent. While moving the right foot forward,
move the right palm down and back to the waist side in a
curve. Swing the left palm from above forward to the front
of the body (Fig. 2-109).

Step with the right foot and jump up, raising the left
leg, knee bent and shank close to the body. At the same
time, push the right palm forward in an arc from the inner
side of the left arm. Swing the left arm backward along
with it, right shoulder extended forward. Turn the head to
the left, eyes left (Fig. 2-110).

Land the right foot, and step with the left foot forward
immediately, toes turned inward. Move the right foot

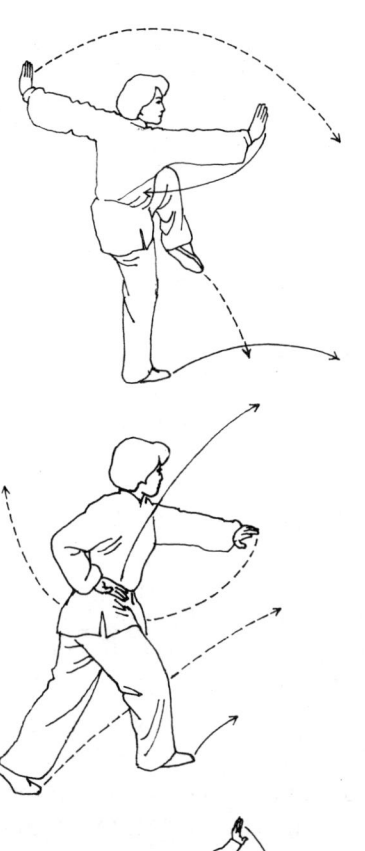

Fig. 2-108

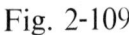
Fig. 2-109

Fig. 2-110

69

another step forward immediately, toes turned outward. Turn the body to the right, drop the right arm and swing it backward. Swing the left arm forward from below (Figs. 2-111, 112).

Step with the right foot and jump up. At the same time, kick with the left leg forward to the upper right and swing the arms upward. Hit the left palm with the back of the right hand over the head. Turn the upper part of the body to the right (Fig. 2-113).

Swing the right leg outward, pat the right instep with both hands, first the left and then the right. Keep the left leg bent at the knee or straight, and place it by the body. Lean the upper part of the body slightly forward. Eyes on the hands (Fig. 2-114).

Essentials: Move in a curved line. While stepping with right foot, turn the toes outward, and landing from heel to toe. In jumping, turn the left leg inside, swing the right leg outward in the shape of a fan. Lean the upper part of the body slightly forward, and slap the instep accurately and loudly. While slapping, bend the left leg and withdraw it to the inner side of the right leg, or keep the leg straight and swing it to the left side of the body. While completing the movements, attention should be paid to the close coordination among the movements of jumping, waist relaxing, body turning, kicking and swinging.

Butterfly

Move the right foot backward and both legs slightly bent. Raise the right arm to the side of the body, bend the left arm at the knee and raise it horizontally in front of the body (Fig. 2-115).

Bend the right leg slightly to support the body, swing the left leg backward to below the hips. Move the left palm back to the front of the right shoulder, and swing the right arm backward. Shift the body weight backward, stamp the

Fig. 2-111

Fig. 2-112

Fig. 2-113

Fig. 2-114

ground with the right foot and skip half a step backward. Land the left foot immediately behind, legs bent, and lean the upper part of the body forward (Figs. 2-116, 117).

Turn the upper part of the body horizontally to the left, body bent forward, shifting the body weight to the left leg. Step with the right leg and quickly swing it backward and upward, instep flat. Swing both arms to the left horizontally at the same time. Eyes on the left (Figs. 2-118, 119).

Continue to turn the body to the left backward, upper body bent forward. After stamping with the left foot, swing it backward and upward, continue to swing the right leg upward with the arms to the left. Eyes front (Fig. 2-120).

Essentials: Bend the body in the air and turn it around horizontally to the left 360 degrees. Keep the chest out, and extend the buttocks. Waist twisting, arm swinging, foot stamping and leg swinging should be well-coordinated.

8. Tumbling Exercises

Tumbling exercises are good for improving the stability of the vestibular organs, and the physical qualities of coordination, nimbleness, speed and power. Following is a description of three tumbling exercises for the beginners·

Straight Body Drop

Stand with feet together, body upright, turn the arms outward and elbow bent. Move the arms to the front of the chest, clench the fists, fist centre inward, eyes front. Lift the heels quickly, straighten the body and fall forward (Fig. 2-121).

Keep the body straight with the outer sides of the forearms on the ground, elbows bent about 90 degrees (Fig. 2-122).

Essentials: Keep the body straight when falling forward,

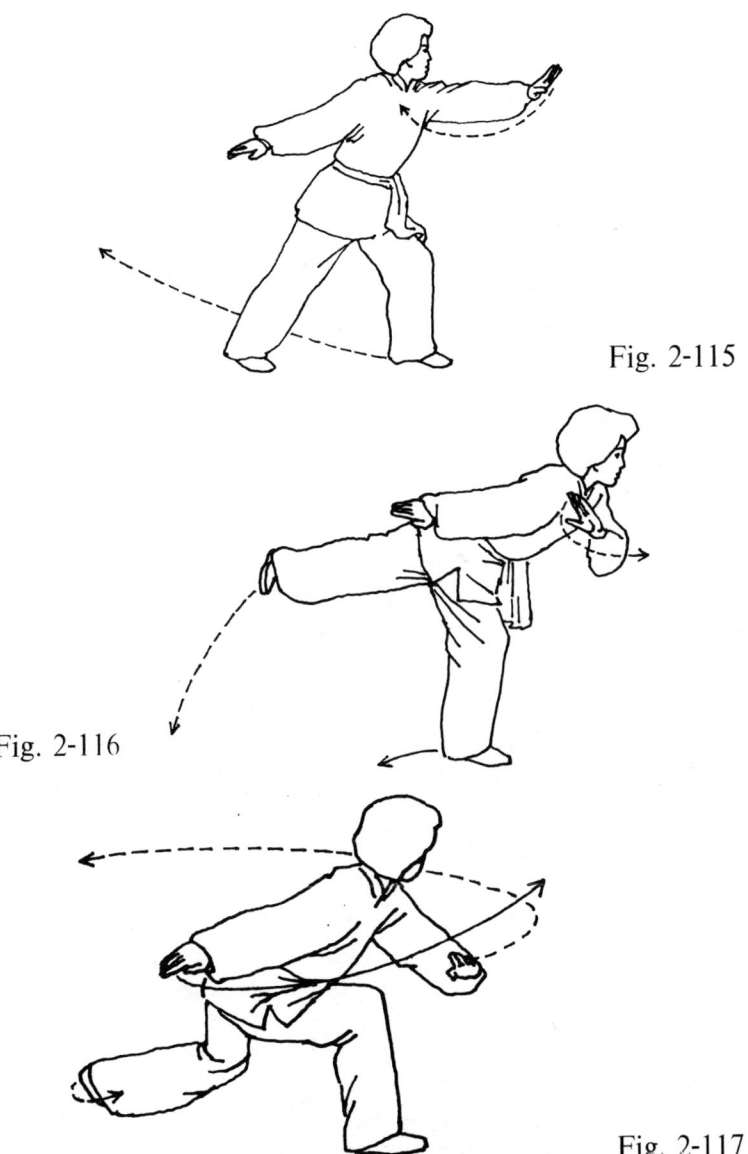

Fig. 2-115

Fig. 2-116

Fig. 2-117

Fig. 2-118   Fig. 2-119

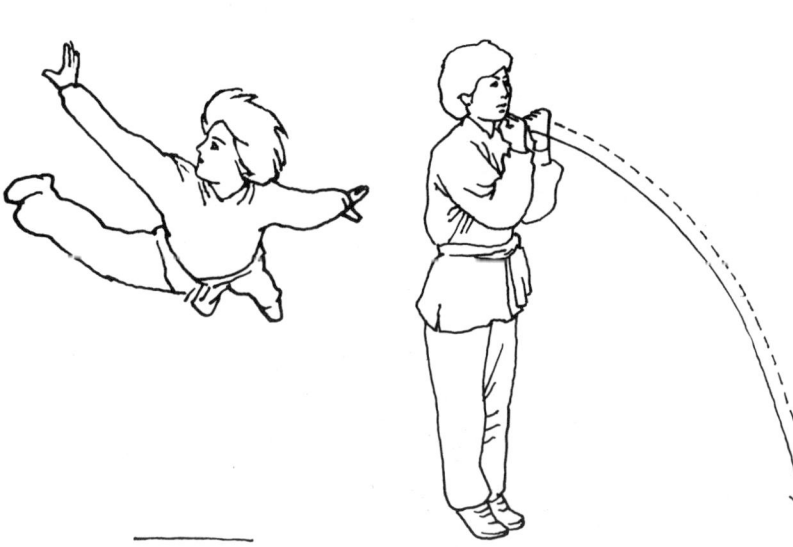

Fig. 2-120   Fig. 2-121

Fig. 2-122

and the buttocks in.

Shoulder Roll

Bend the left leg at the knee, right heel off the ground. Bend the upper part of the body forward, and extend the left arm forward, elbow slightly bent. Eyes on the left hand (Fig. 2-123).

Move the right foot forward. Continue to bend the upper part of the body forward, and bow the head. Bend the right arm at elbow and place the forearm on the ground, both heels off the ground (Fig. 2-124).

Lower the head and withdraw it, roll forward on the right shoulder and back, and swing the left leg upward. Continue to roll forward, body tucked, and the left arm on ground (Figs. 2-125, 126).

Essentials: Roll on the ground on the shoulder, back, waist and hips, in order. The movements must be round and quick. Rise swiftly.

Fig. 2-123

Fig. 2-124

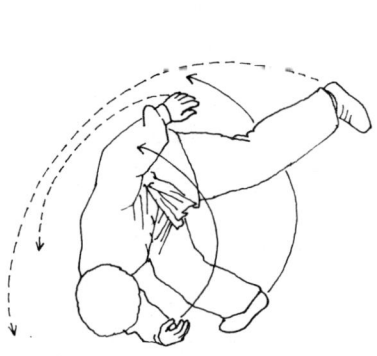

Fig. 2-125

Fig. 2-126

Carp Jump

Lie on the back, bend the body by swinging the legs upward, hands on the knees. Kick the ground with both legs, thrust the stomach out and jump up (Figs. 2-127, 128).

Essentials: Keep the body bent backward in a semicircle, feet apart to twice the shoulder breadth. Kicking and jumping should be swift and coordinated.

9. Exercises for Principal Movements

Punch with Bow Step

This is one of the most basic movements in *Chang Quan*. It is also a basic stance for many other fist and weapon exercises. For example, the method of using power in thrusting broadsword, sword and spear with bow step is similar to that for punching with bow step. The movement

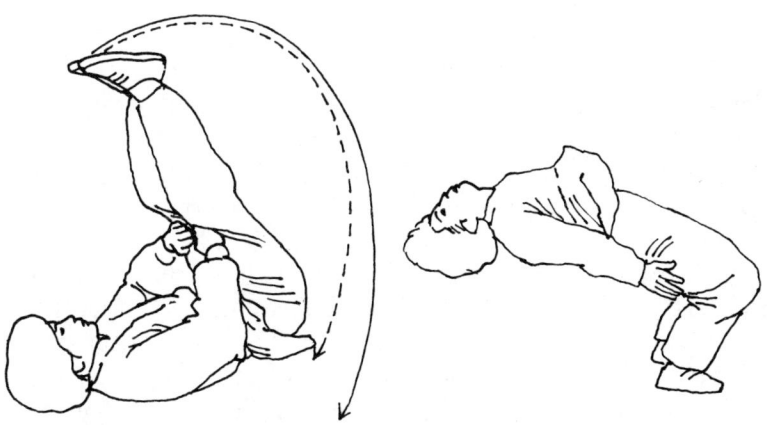

Fig. 2-127   Fig. 2-128

of punching with bow step is not complicated, nor difficult for beginners. But if the movements are to be executed correctly and powerfully, they require constant practice.

Punching the right fist with the left bow step or punching the left fist with the right bow step are both called punching with bow step. Following is a description of the punching with the forward bow step (advance) to facilitate the integration of the combination exercises and routine exercises.

1) Descriptions

1. Stand with feet together, keep all fingers of both hands together, arms straight, and close to the outer sides of the legs. Eyes front (Fig. 2-129).

2. Stand with feet together. Keep both hands clenched in fists, elbows bent, and hold them by the waist, fist centres up. Eyes left (Fig. 2-130).

3. Lower the body, move the left foot forward to the left, toes turned outward. Bend both legs to a half squat to form a half horse-riding step. Bend the left arm at elbow and move it upward and past the left chest to block to the left (Fig. 2-131).

4. Turn the body to the left and shift the body weight forward. Bend the left leg to a half squat, and straighten the right leg powerfully to form a left bow step. At the same time, punch the right fist forward quickly and move the left fist back to the waist side, relax the waist and extend the shoulders. Eyes front (Fig. 2-132).

5. Turn the left foot outward, shift the body weight to the left leg, bend the legs to a half squat, and move the right foot forward at the same time. Turn the upper part of the body slightly to the left, without changing the form and stance (Fig. 2-133). Straighten the left leg to form a bow step, and thrust the left fist forward. The movement is the same as for 4. The only difference is between left

and right.

2) How to Practice

1. Practice the bow step without changing place. Use the legs alternately. Grasp the basic requirements of the bow step.

2. Keep doing the exercises for moving the foot forward to change the half horse-riding step into the bow step. Attention should be paid to straightening the rear leg and pressing the outer side of the foot down, turning the waist. At the same time, keep both legs bent at the knees while advancing, with the upper part of the body erect. Also, relax the shoulders and drop the buttocks. The number of repetitions depends on the practitioner's own condition, but careful attention should be paid to the movements and posture of the upper part of the body (Figs. 2-134, 135).

3. Practise punching in the same position (Figs. 2-59,

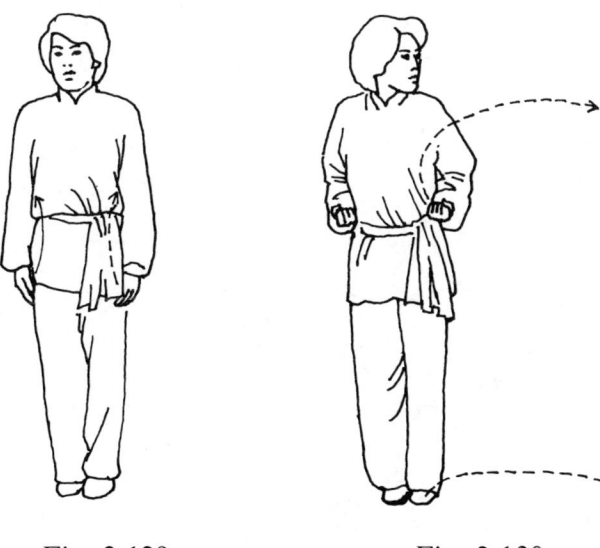

Fig. 2-129   Fig. 2-130

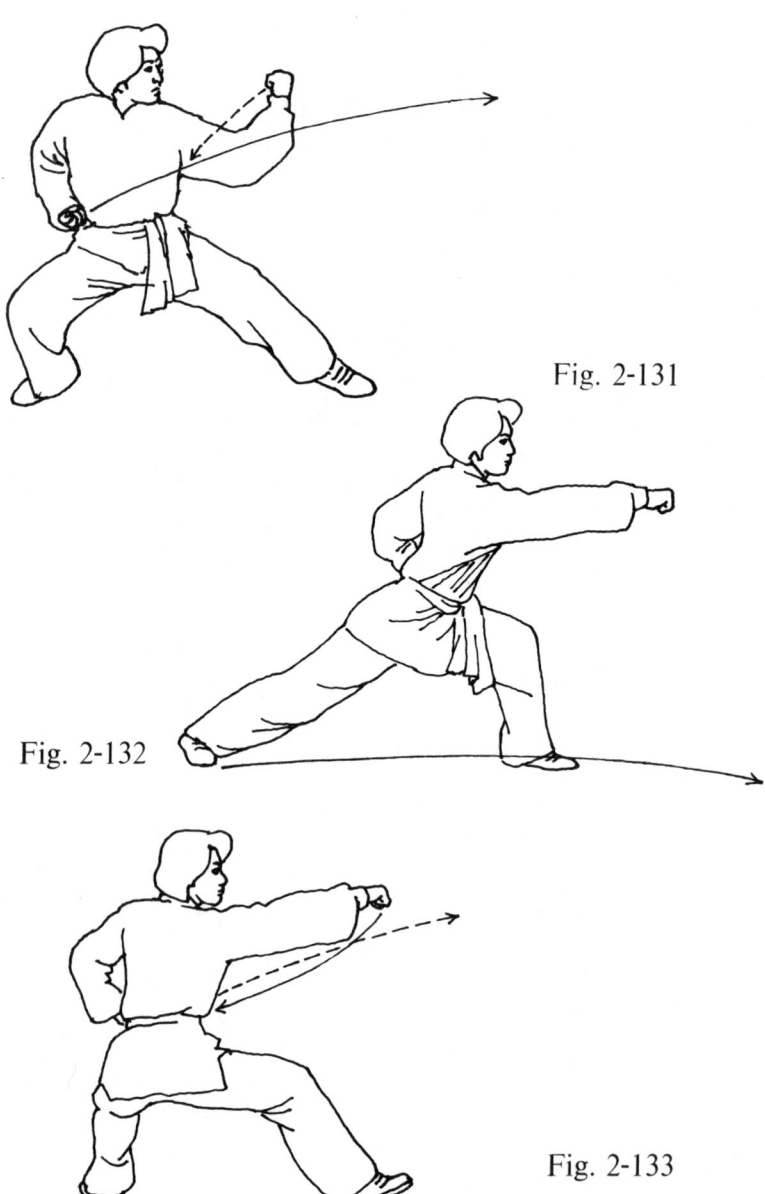

Fig. 2-131

Fig. 2-132

Fig. 2-133

2-60). In doing the punching exercises: (1) thrust the fist forward with the aid of the power from turning the waist and buttocks; (2) twist the waist and extend the shoulders forward so as to thrust the fist further forward and more powerfully; (3) relax the shoulders and drop the elbows, so as to deliver the power through the shoulders and elbows to the fists; (4) while thrusting the fist, keep the forearm tightly close to the waist side, and extend the elbow quickly and closely by the ribs. Turn the fist and forearm inward quickly when the elbow is almost off the ribs, fist centre down or fist eye up. This is intended to effectively prevent the turning over of the elbow while thrusting the fist, and avoid application of power to inaccurate points.

When withdrawing the fist: (1) first pull back the elbow joint, bend the elbow and move it back to the waist side. (2) while bending the elbow and moving it back, turn the

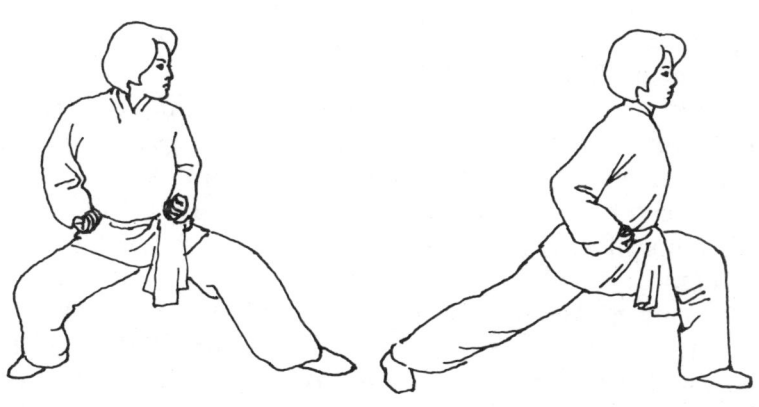

Fig. 2-134   Fig. 2-135

fist and forearm outward into the fist-holding position.

4. Practise the complete movements. At the beginning, the movement should not be practised too quickly; it should be done slowly according to the basic requirements. After you have skillfully grasped the process of the movement, gradually increase the speed and power of fist thrusting.

3) Common Mistakes and Corrections

1. Punching the fist and forming the bow step are not completed at the same time.

A beginner is apt to punch the fist while moving his foot forward. As a result, the fist is quickly thrust forward while the bow step is slowly completed. Therefore, in the process of forming the half horse-riding step between the forward step and the bow step, the posture of the upper part of the body should remain unchanged. Then straighten the leg and punch, so that the two movements are finished at the same time.

2. The rise and fall of the body are too extreme in the forward move.

Attention should be paid on the following two points in correcting this mistake: (1) while advancing, just keep the rear leg in the fixed bent knee position so as to control the level of the body weight; (2) before advancing, the front foot should be turned outward with its heel as axis. Then shift the body weight and bend the knee for support.

3. Leaning the upper part of the body too far forward, resulting in the heel or outer side of the rear foot off the ground.

Do more exercises as described in No. 2 in How to Practice. Moreover, keep the basic posture of the upper part of the body: head upright, neck erect, chest out, and waist and buttocks dropped.

4. Shrugging both shoulders, thus affecting the power

and speed in punching.

Do more punching exercises at the same place to consciously overcome the erroneous movements of shrugging and raising the elbow, and increase the speed step by step.

Thread Palm with Crouch Step

This is a common movement in the footwork exercises of *Chang Quan*. It is intended to increase the interest of beginners and overcome the fatigue and dullness in practising a certain stance through symmetry between left and right and constant changes in the footwork. At the same time, it gives beginners an opportunity to repeatedly practise three palm techniques (pressing, piercing and snapping). It also increases the strength of their legs, and improves the pliability of hip and ankle joints, as well as coordination between upper and lower limbs. In recent years, with the improvement of the Wushu routine demonstration skills, the routine movements have become more varied. Therefore, Thread Palm with Crouch Step is not only a simple exercise for the footwork and palm techniques, but is often present in the routines as a process movement; this serves as a connecting link between movements. There are left and right movements in the Thread Palm with Crouch Step. They should be practised alternately and repeatedly.

Following is a description of the Thread Palm with Crouch Step, which is simple and easy for any beginner.

1) Description

1. Stand with feet together and keep fingers together and arms straight against the outer sides of the legs. Eyes front (Fig. 2-129).

2. Turn the body to the right, bend the right leg to a half squat. Move the left foot backward, and straighten the leg to form a bow step. Bend the right arm at elbow and

move it to the waist side, palm face up. Swing the left palm from left upward and forward and then to the front of the body, palm obliquely down. Eyes front (Fig. 2-136).

Essentials: Keep the left arm straight and move it down by the ear to the front of the body. Relax and drop the shoulders and twist the waist to the right, so as to extend the palm further forward.

3. Thread the right palm forward above the back of the left palm, arm straight, palm face up. Move the left palm back to under the right arm. Eyes on the right palm (Fig. 2-137).

Essentials: Straighten the right arm forcefully. Apply power to the finger tips while threading the palm. Relax the left shoulder.

4. Turn the body to the left and bend the right leg to full squat to form a left crouch step, right knee and toes outward. Straighten the left leg, toes inward and the whole

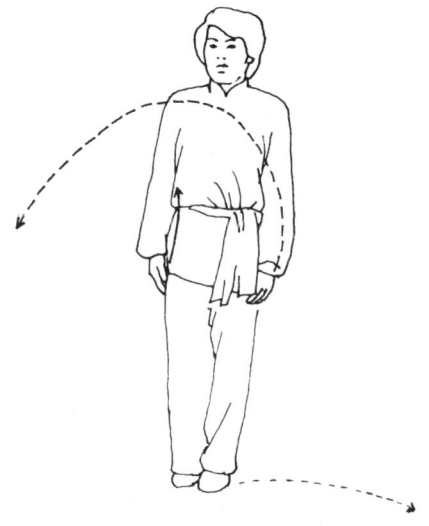

Fig. 2-129

foot on the ground. Move the left palm downward while turning the body, and thread it forward. Raise the right arm obliquely upward to the right side of the body, palm facing forward. Turn the head to the left at the same time. Eyes look ahead to the left (Fig. 2-138).

Essentials: Bend the upper part of the body to the right leg before turning the body. Keep the left palm fingers forward and close to the upper part of the body. Thread the left palm along the inner side of the left leg, power to the finger tips. Keep the chest out and forward, right side of the waist slightly raised.

5. Straighten the right leg forcefully, and bend the left leg to form a bow step. When the left palm is moved further forward and upward and threaded to the front of the body, turn both wrists upward to form upright palms, right palm slightly higher than the left. Eyes on the left palm (Fig. 2-139).

Essentials: Continue to thread the left palm forward with no stop, and turn the wrist up to form an upright palm after the right leg is straightened. Drop the waist, and seat the hips when the crouch step is changed into the bow step with the body weight shifted forward. Keep the upper part of the body upright and avoid raising the buttocks and falling forward.

6. Turn the upper part of the body slightly to the left. Move the right palm from above the top of the head forward and press it down in front of the body, palm centre down. Bend the left arm at the elbow and withdraw the palm to the side of the waist, palm centre up. Eyes front (Fig. 2-140).

Essentials: The same as illustrated in Fig. 2-136.

The points for attention for the Palm Threading with Right Crouch Step are the same as described above in Nos. 3, 4 and 5. The only difference is between the left and the

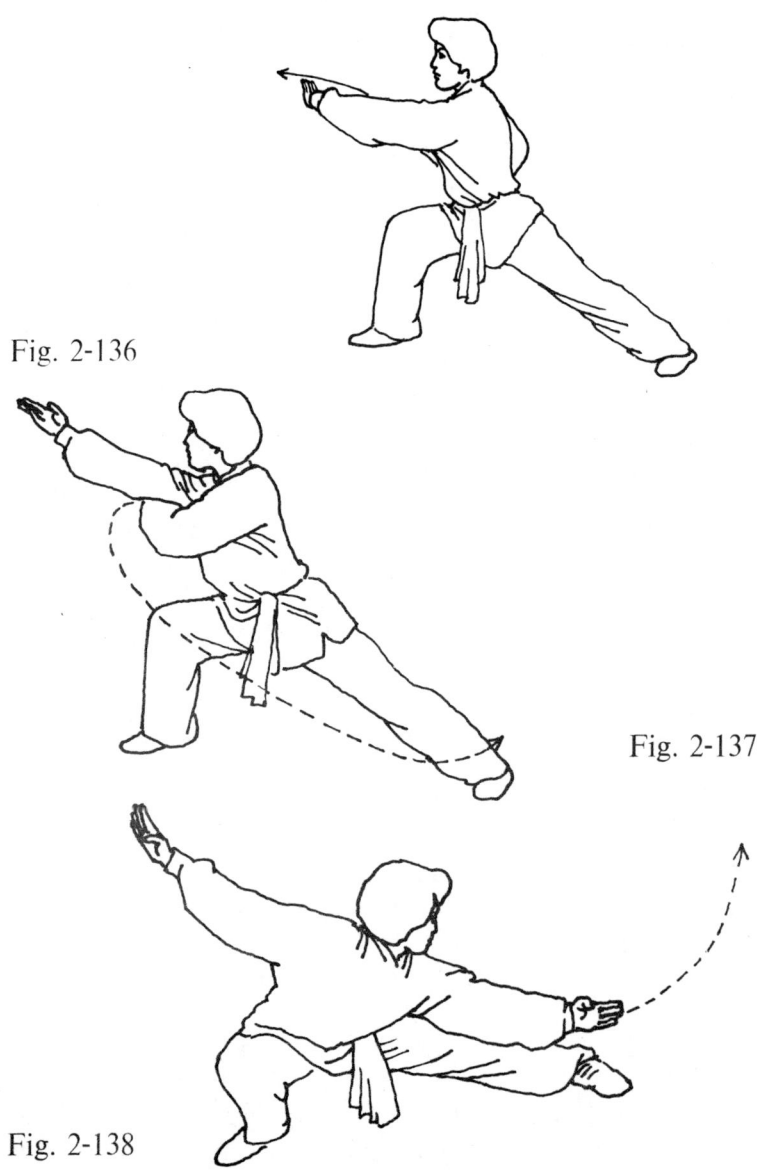

Fig. 2-136

Fig. 2-137

Fig. 2-138

Fig. 2-139

Fig. 2-140

right movements.

2) Basic Methods for Practice

In learning every new movement, beginners should first know the line of movement, movement specifications and requirements, and then do some physical training so as to lay down a good foundation for learning and grasping the basic movements.

1. Leg stretch with crouch step

Bend the right leg to full squat, knee and toes slightly outward, buttocks close to the shank. Keep the left leg straight and close to the ground, toes inward, both feet on the ground. Put the right hand on the right knee and left hand on the left knee. Exert force to stretch the legs. (See Fig. 2-16. The only difference is between the left and right directions.) If you have sore muscles, just change the left crouch step to the right crouch step. At the same time, keep the waist erect, buttocks relaxed and chest out when pressing the legs down. Constant practice helps to improve the pliability and flexibility of your hip and ankle joints and legs.

2. Exercises for the changeover between the two different stances

Put both hands on the hips. First practise the bow step and then change to crouch step, and then straighten the leg to do the bow step again. Repeat the exercises—bow step—crouch step—bow step. Perform both left and right movements by changing the legs. Do the exercises according to the specifications for the two different stances. Keep the body balanced. Be careful to avoid straightening the legs and standing up before changing the crouch step to the bow step. The process of changing speed should be properly slowed so as to improve the coordination upon turning the waist, and bending and straightening the legs.

3. Palms threading at the same place

The exercises for the upper limbs are the same as illustrated in Figs. 2-136, 137 and 138. Do the exercises alternately between the left and the right. It is essential to understand the extending force in straightening the arm with the right palm which was first threaded, and relaxing the shoulders and threading the left palm to the left. Both arms should be extended as fully as possible at both sides.

4. Do the exercises for the complete Palm Threading with Crouch Step movements.

3) Common Mistakes and Corrections

1. The shoulder of the threading arm (right arm) is often to be turned while changing the bow step to the crouch step.

This mistake is often seen in executing the movements illustrated in Figs. 2-137 and 138. The palm centre should be forward, if done incorrectly, unnecessary movements occur. To correct this mistake, you should: (1) extend the fingers of both hands fully to both sides while threading the palms; (2) turn the forearm inward for the first threading arm, and change the palm centre up to palm centre forward. No changes in the directions for the shoulders and elbows are necessary.

2. The left palm is far away from the body in the course of threading.

The main cause for this mistake is straightening the arm too early without extending the fingers forward enough in threading the palm. When practising, you should first move the elbow to the left, backward, to direct the fingers forward in threading the left palm downward. Then thread the palm forward to the left, arm straight, with power on the finger tips. Both the left palm and arm should be close to the inner side of the left leg.

3. The range of movement is small.

To execute the complete movements well, there should be a semicircle. Many beginners often make straight falls and rises because the range of movement is small.

Straight fall—Thrusting the chest out to form the crouch step before bending the upper part of the body to bow leg. Beginners should first bend the chest forward to the bow leg and then continue to execute the crouch step. They can also consciously bow their heads to help bend the chest forward.

Straight rise—Straightening both legs at the same time and rising after threading the palm with the crouch step. The common cause for this mistake is the failure to grasp the essentials and the shortage of leg power. A beginner should first extend the left hand further than the left foot after threading the left palm, and then bend the left leg and straighten the right leg. Moreover, he can also place a small obstacle, or ask an assistant to place a straight arm above where the beginner is to thread the palm. This will make him conscious of moving his palm forward under something, and he will understand the range of movement and the feeling of his own body. Repeated practice helps to increase the power of the legs and correct the mistake.

Another important point: at the beginning, a beginner should do the exercises slowly. Only in this way can he learn the essentials of a movement and how to apply the power in the movement. After the skills are improved, he can increase the speed of the movement. This helps you to learn the complete movement well and acquire a correct pattern for the movement. In fact, Palm Threading with Crouch Step should not be executed too fast.

Backward Sweep with Hand Stand

Leg sweep is one of the sweeping leg techniques in the

Chang Quan exercises. It is very common in the routine performances. It is fast and highly technical. It covers a wide range and requires good skills. It can be used for attack and defence. This exercise can help to increase the power and pliability of the waist, hips, knees and ankles, and improve the coordination of different body parts. Leg sweep exercises include forward sweep with straight body, forward sweep with hand stand, backward sweep with hand stand, and half backward sweep with hand stand.

1) Descriptions
The same as the leg exercises described for Figs. 2-43, 44, 45, 46.

2) Technical Essentials
1. In the course of sweeping, the right leg should be extended backward, knee straight and heel on the ground.
2. Bend the left leg to full squat, keep the waist erect and hips dropped, and avoid having the buttocks raised.
3. Twist the waist and swing the hips. Sweep and turn swiftly.
4. Turn the body, hands on the ground. The sweeping should be continuous and well-coordinated.

3) How to Practice
1. Choose a level ground before doing the exercises, and do the warm-ups well. The important thing is to relax the joints of the lower limbs in order to avoid injuries like pulled muscles and sprains.
2. Improve the pliability of the hips, knees and ankle joints by stretching the legs with the crouch step. A beginner can use the hands to press each knee joint respectively, for the leg stretch. Pause for a certain period of time after pressing down to the crouch stance. When the legs and ankle joints are sore and painful, pause for a few minutes or continue to execute the leg stretch (Fig.

2-16). In executing the crouch stance, straighten the right leg, toes inward, with whole foot on the ground. Keep the chest out and waist dropped. With improvement of the pliability of the joints, you can also use both hands to hold the right foot to increase the degree of difficulty in executing the crouch stance; this will also improve the pliability of the waist. Leg stretch can also be executed with the bow step. While pressing for the stretch, keep the upper part of the body erect and hips dropped, straighten the rear leg and raise the heel properly.

3. Repeatedly practice the crouch stance with hands on the ground. After learning the movement as shown in Fig. 2-43, you can raise the legs slightly to the upper left, and change to the crouch stance. Put both hands on the ground, as shown in Fig. 2-44, to increase the range of swing and power for twisting the waist to the right backward. Through this practice, you will learn the essentials of the movements of bending the body, twisting the waist and putting hands on the ground to support the body. This will improve the pliability of the waist and hips, as well as the speed of the movements.

4. Learn the backward sweep. If you have not yet grasped the technical essentials well, you can start with a semicircular sweep, and then gradually increase the degree of the sweep. After you have grasped the essentials, you can start to do the full sweep (360 degrees). You must proceed step by step according to the correct technical essentials.

5. Ask an assistant to help you to understand the technical essentials. The assistant is advised to stand obliquely behind your right leg, bending his knees slightly and body forward, and holding your right ankle joint with his right hand (Fig. 2-141). One way is to walk slowly behind you and hold your right leg to turn and sweep

slowly. Another method is to stand at the same place and push your right leg to increase force and speed when you start to sweep with the right leg.

4) Common Mistakes and Corrections

1. The heel of the right foot is off the ground in the course of the sweeping.

During the practice be sure to turn the toes of the right foot inward and press the outer side of the foot downward forcefully. At the same time, shift the body weight slightly to the right leg so as to increase the power of the right foot in sweeping the ground.

2. The range of the sweep is small (you rise while sweeping).

Keep the body weight down in the course of sweeping and the buttocks close to the left heel. Extend the right leg backward to the right as fully as possible and swing the leg

Fig. 2-141

and hips.

3. The locations of both supporting hands are incorrect.

Apart from repeatedly practising the movement as shown in Fig. 2-44 and putting the hands back on the ground, you should continue to do the exercises to improve the pliability of the waist, hips, knees and ankles. Push the left shoulder forcefully to the right to help twist the upper part of the body to the right and determine the correct positions for the supporting hands.

4. The backward sweep is less than 360 degrees.

On the one hand, do more exercises as described in No. 3, to increase the degree of waist twisting. Place emphasis on coordination in twisting the waist, turning the head backward and swinging the hips, while sweeping the right leg. On the other hand, continue to turn the upper part of the body backward to the right.

5. The sweep is too slow.

While stress is put on twisting the waist and shaking the head, it is necessary to increase the starting speed of the right leg sweep. Refrain from starting the sweep after the hands are placed firmly on the ground. The sweep should be started at the same time you are placing the hands on the ground.

In addition, you can also do the exercise shown in Fig. 2-141. Ask an assistant to help you to increase the starting speed.

Kick-Up

Kick-up is one of the balance movements in Wushu, and is common in the *Chang Quan* competition routines. Among powerful and swift rolls, rises and falls, the clean and neat kick-up movements give people a feeling of forcefulness, gracefulness and vigor. Kick-up exercises help to improve the pliability of the leg muscles and ligaments, increase the range of movement of the hip joints and raise the lifting power of the legs and the balancing ability of the body. With kick-up as the base, you can continue to improve the control ability of the legs and execute the high leg-raising balance and other movements with a higher degree of difficulty. In doing the kick-up exercises, you can use either leg. Following is a description of the kick-up exercises with the right leg.

1) Description

1. Stand with feet together, arms naturally down by both sides of the body. Eyes front (Fig. 2-129).

2. Stand on the left leg to support the body, bend the right leg at knee and raise it, ankle joint flexed. Place the right arm against the inner side of the thigh, hold the right outer ankle bone and heel with the right hand, left arm naturally swinging to the left side, upper part of the body upright (Fig. 2-142).

3. Stand firmly with the left leg supporting the body, hold up the right leg to the upper right with the right hand. Kick-up with the right leg and straighten it, ankle joint flexed, foot sole up and both legs straight. Raise the left hand and flash the palm above the head to the left. Keep the chest out and head up. Eyes front (Fig. 2-20).

2) How to Practice

Good pliability is required for the kick-up exercises. Therefore, the first item should be an exercise for the kicking leg stretch, and then other exercises for gradual improvement.

1. Leg stretch and leg press.

In executing the front leg stretch, you should straighten both legs, keep the waist erect, hips in, and bend the upper part of the body forward and downward. Place the hands on the knee; when you find it sore, just pause for a while. You can also hold the feet with both hands for leg stretch exercises (Figs. 2-11, 12).

Side leg stretch. Keep the toes of the supporting leg forward, and put the other leg on an object with a certain height, ankle joint flexed. Raise the hand on the other side of the supporting leg and bend the body sideways to stretch the upper leg. Keep the hips open and extend the raising hand to behind the head. With improvement in pliability, you can raise the height for the stretching leg (Fig. 2-13).

Besides, you can also ask an assistant to help you to do the stretch exercise. For example, the front leg press (Fig. 2-19), and side leg press (Fig. 2-21). The amount of power and height should be different for different people. The general principle is to increase them step by step. Do avoid acting with undue haste and causing unnecessary muscle and ligament injuries.

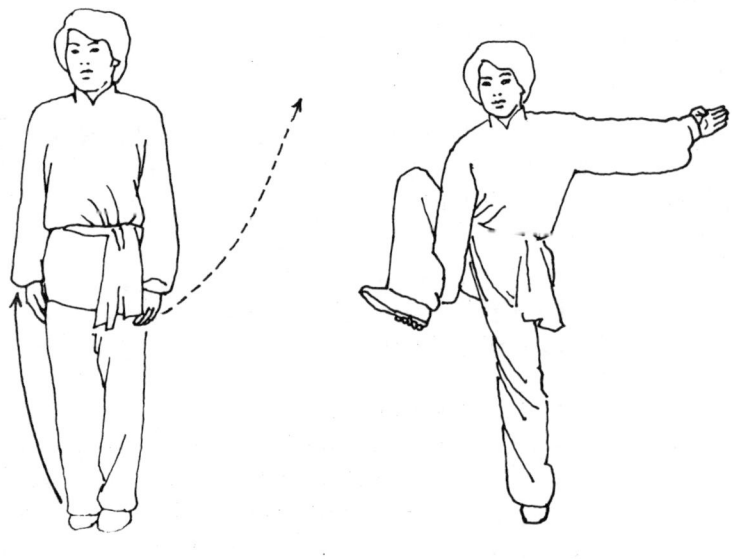

Fig. 2-129   Fig. 2-142

2. Side kick

Do the side kick exercises after the leg stretch and press. Combination of stretch and kick helps to improve pliability, nimbleness and control power of the legs. In executing the side kick, you should open the hips, and turn the toes of the left leg forward or slightly outward. The upper part of the body should be turned sidewards, then kick up with the right leg towards the shoulder, left arm swung upward and shoulders relaxed (Figs 2-27, 28).

3. Knee raising with leg hold

Stand on the left leg, bend the right leg and raise it. Hold the knee joint and the outer side of the foot with the hands, respectively, with chest out and waist erect. Eyes front (Fig. 2-143). When you find the supporting leg sore, straighten the leg forcefully and as long as possible. Do the exercises with alternate legs.

4. Kick-up exercises

(1) Put one hand on an object for support, and use the other hand to execute the right leg movement as shown in Fig. 2-20. Then gradually reduce the power of the auxiliary support and change to one-leg support. (2) At the beginning, the kick may not be as high as you desire often due to poor pliability. However, with improvement in pliability, you will surely increase the height for the leg press. Therefore, beginners are not advised to be over anxious for early success. Do not increase the height blindly without due attention to correct posture and other requirements.

3) Common Mistakes and Corrections

1. The legs are not straight.

Generally, this is because the legs are not pliable enough. On the one hand, you should improve the pliability through stretch, kick and press exercises, and put stress on the straightening of the legs; on the other, you should not do exercises for high stretch and high press movements before requirements for pliability are met.

2. Bending the upper part of the body side forward.

That is to say, the upper part of the body between the front and side stretch legs. The first cause for the mistake is the failure to grasp the essentials; the second, poor pliability. This problem should draw your attention at the very beginning to do the stretch. Kick and press exercises. The toes of the supporting leg should be forward or slightly outward. The raised leg should move upward powerfully behind the shoulder on the same side, with the hip joint relaxed and pushed forward. Swing the arm on the other side upward forcefully behind the head, shoulder relaxed and extended backward. Don't relax the waist or bend forward or raise the buttocks backward.

3. Failure to hook the foot.

(1) Follow the requirements for hooking the foot. (2) Do more exercises to improve the elasticity and pliability of the ankle joint and the shank muscles. Sit on the ground, feet together and straight, hold the balls of the feet with both hands and pull them back forcefully towards the body and relax. Repeat. Also, stand erect with one foot hooked, tightly pressed against the wall. Then straighten both legs, push the hip joints forward forcefully and repeatedly, the number of repetitions depending on your own condition.

4. Standing unsteadily.

In executing the kick-up, keep all five toes of the supporting leg against the ground. A beginner should have an assistant help him so as to acquire the feeling of balance. In short, you should keep the waist erect, neck upright, head raised and eyes front.

Side Sole Kick

Side sole kick is a leg technique for flexion and extension. It is good for improving the pliability, nimbleness and control ability of the legs. It also helps to demonstrate a certain level of training for the legs. This movement is characterized by a fast start, powerful release of force, nimbleness and unexpectedness. It can be used for attack and defence; therefore, it is a common leg technique.

Side sole kick can be executed either on the right side or on the left side. Because the requirements are the same for this exercise with either leg, here is a description only of the side sole kick with the left leg.

1) Description

1. Stand with feet together, and keep fingers together and arms straight, close to the outer sides of the legs. Eyes front (Fig. 2-129).

2. Cross the hands in front of the body, right hand on the left, and palm centre inward. Move both hands forward and upward to over the head in a curve, arms slightly bent and palm centres forward. Eyes front (Fig. 2-144).

3. Shift the body weight to the left and move the right foot obliquely forward in front of the left foot, toes outward. Bend both legs to a cross, left heel off the ground, body weight between the legs. Move the hands sidewards, and downward and upward, respectively, in a curved line. Cross them in front of the body and bend the wrists into standing palms and rest them in front of the chest. Turn the head to the left while bending the wrists. Eyes left front (Fig. 2-145).

4. Stand on the right foot, bend the left leg at knee and raise it to the left side. Then extend the left leg, foot hooked and turned inward, and kick upward forcefully to the left side, power on the heel. At the same time, push the hands out respectively to both sides, palm centres obliquely down, fingers forward, power on the outer edges of the hands. Lean the upper part of the body obliquely to

the right. Eyes on the left foot (Fig. 2-146).

2) Technical Essentials

1. Release the force powerfully with accurate force points.

A beginner should, first of all, learn the line of movement in the side sole kick. There must be a process of fist bending and then extending the leg, first slowly and then quickly. Both the power and speed in kicking should be increased gradually, so as to make the force points accurate.

2. Extend the hips and thrust the abdomen out fully while kicking. As every practitioner has different pliability, one should determine his own height for the side kick, depending on his own condition. Beginners usually practise the low kick (to the knee level) or horizontal kick (to the waist level). Gradually increase the kicking height on the basis of extending the hips and thrusting the abdomen. Avoid acting with undue haste.

3. Coordination between side sole kick and push palm.

There are two points to make. First, side sole kick and push palm should be completed at the same time. There should be the feeling that both the upper and lower limbs (left leg and right palm) are pushed forward; second, in the preparatory form preceding the side sole kick (Fig. 2-145), there must be "relaxation." Both the shoulders and elbows should be relaxed, the legs naturally bent and together. Do not bend the upper part of the body forward too much for the sake of generating the desired power.

3) How to Practice

For a beginner, there is some difficulty in executing the side sole kick well. Before your physical ability reaches a desired level, it is hard to avoid injuring the body if you insist on doing this fairly fast and high movement. In order to avoid muscle and ligament injuries, you should

Fig. 2-143　　　　　Fig. 2-129　　　　　Fig. 2-144

Fig. 2-145　　　　　Fig. 2-146

perform sufficient warm-up exercises, so as to prepare the physiological functions of the muscles to suit the needs of the activity. After that, you should proceed to do stretch and kick exercises to improve the pliability and muscular power and extend the range of the movement of the joints. There are many ways to practise. Here are descriptions of only some:

1. Horizontal cross

Put the hands on the ground for support, shake the hips up and down slowly to place the inner sides of both legs gradually close to the ground (Fig. 2-23).

2. Side leg stretch

Stand on the left leg, toes forward and place the right leg on an object to the waist level, leg straight, foot hooked and toes up. Bend the upper part of the body sideways to the right leg (Fig. 2-13). Or keep the left toes forward and repeatedly bend and straighten the right knee, without swinging the trunk. Hold the knee joints with the hands.

3. Some people fail to raise their kicking leg, not entirely because the pliability of the kicking leg is insufficient but, in some degree, because the ligaments of the supporting leg are not pliable enough. Therefore, on the basis of Fig. 2-13, you can raise the height of the stretching leg and execute the high leg stretch (Fig. 2-14). On the one hand, this helps to increase the need for the pliability of the left leg; on the other, it intensifies the training of the supporting leg.

4. The effective method to improve the power and pliability of the muscles is to combine the leg stretch with kicking. After the leg stretch, do the exercises for the side sole kick with the forward step.

5. Do separate exercises for the major movements of the lower limbs.

Place both hands on an object, raise the left leg, and

first bend it and then straighten it. Do this first slowly and then quickly, first at a low level and then at a higher level. This will help you understand the line of movement, the direction of kicking, and the order for the release of force (Figs. 2-147, 148). You can also ask an assistant to help you to do the exercise.

6. In doing the push palm exercise in the same position, the arm is also first bent and then straightened. Both hands must have the power to push the palms forward. At the same time, relax the shoulders. Finally, do the exercises for the complete side sole kick.

4) Common Mistakes and Corrections

1. Bending the upper part of the body forward too much, with the hips not fully extended. To correct this mistake, first, do more exercises to improve pliability; second, consciously uplift the trunk and slant to the right

Fig. 2-147   Fig. 2-148

side. The trunk, arms and legs should be at the same level.

2. Raising the left leg straight and swinging it upward. The main cause for this mistake is failure to grasp the essentials well. Keep doing the exercise in Figs. 2-147, 148.

Turn the Waist Over

Turn the waist over is a principal movement in the exercises for the waist in *Chang Quan*. It is very common in the routine performance. As this movement calls for shoulder relaxation, arm swinging and smooth power, the body weight is lowered, and the waist, hips and chest are fully extended when the waist is twisted. This fully demonstrates the wide range and high speed. Therefore, the exercises for turning the waist over help to improve the pliability of the waist and hips, as well as the coordination of other body parts.

Turning the waist over exercises include turning the waist over at cross step, at front cross step, with forward step, and with a raised leg. Following is a description of the most basic movement—turning the waist over at cross step.

1) Description

The same as described for the basic skills in Fig. 2-39, and Figs. 2-53, 54, 55.

2) How to Practice

1. Quality preparations

(1) Bending the trunk backward into a bridge. It helps to improve the pliability and flexibility (nimbleness) of the hips, waist and shoulders. A beginner first lies flat on the back, and bends the knees and elbows to place the palms and soles on the ground. He then pushes the hands, kicks the ground and thrusts the chest to rise and fall repeatedly to form bridges (Fig. 2-49). There should be a pause after every rise and fall. At the same time, kick forcefully with

both feet and straighten the knees as much as possible so as to shift the body weight to the hands.

(2) Ask an assistant to help you. Stand face to face with the assistant who holds your waist with both hands while you move up and down (Fig. 2-50), the amount of power depending on how much you can bear.

2. Technical training

(1) After grasping the preparatory form as shown in Fig. 2-39, continue with the exercise as shown in Fig. 2-53. Put the left arm down and swing it to the left to understand the release of force in the swingover of the straight arm.

(2) With the help of the assistant, get to know the movement of the turnover, and the coordination of the arms, waist, chest and head. The assistant should hold the arms of the practitioner with crossed hands, left above and right below, to help him to thrust the chest out, raise the head and keep the body balance (Figs. 2-149, 150, 151).

3) Essential Points

1. A beginner should do the exercise first slowly and then quickly, and learn to understand the line of movement, body posture and coordination between the different parts of the body. Afterwards, gradually increase the speed of the turnover. He can also ask an assistant to help with the left arm in order to start the movement quickly.

2. In turning the waist over, relax the shoulders, extend both arms fully and straighten them. In the course of the turning, the hands, elbows and shoulders should move together. At the same time, the waist should be twisted and turned quickly so as to coordinate with the movements of the upper limbs to increase the speed.

3. The waist should be turned in a vertical circle. Therefore, after executing the movements as shown in Figs. 2-54, 55, you should thrust the chest out and extend

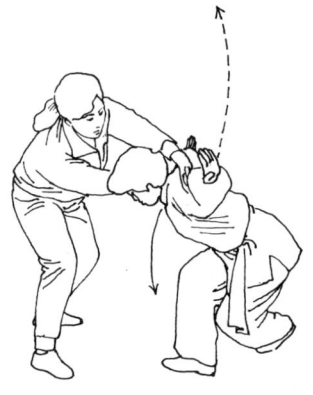

Fig. 2-149

Fig. 2-150

Fig. 2-151

the hips. Bend the head backward and move the arms upward in a vertical circle and close to the body in order to make the movement smooth and fully-extended.

4) Common Mistakes and Corrections

1. The arms cannot be pulled out in turning the waist, and the range of the movement is small.

The main cause for this mistake is that the right hand follows too quickly in the course of the turning. In doing the exercise, stress should be put on the left arm. The right arm should not be moved too quickly, but kept straight by the body side.

2. Rising while turning

The main cause for this is insufficient pliability of the waist and hips. Keep doing exercises which bend the waist forward and backward. Bend the body backward into a bridge and turn the body with the arms swinging to improve pliability and nimbleness. Moreover, ask an assistant to help you understand the essentials of the movements and keep the body weight balanced.

Butterfly

The butterfly is a movement of turning the body in jumping. It is very common in the routines of all Chinese boxing schools. A good grasp of the butterfly helps not only to increase the degree of difficulty of the routines, but also to improve performance and develop the physical qualities of the body, generally. On this basis, you can also continue to do a still more difficult movement—a butterfly with a body turn of 360 degrees.

1) Description

1. Move the left foot forward to the left, legs slightly bent, and trunk slightly turned to the left. At the same time, swing the right arm to the left horizontally, left arm bent at elbow, moving the left palm to under the right

armpit. Both palms face down (Fig. 4-61).

2. Move the right foot forward in front of the left foot, and turn the body to the left at the same time. Swing the right arm to the left backward and then upward in a circle. Swing the left arm horizontally in front of the body to the left side (Fig. 4-62).

3. Continue to turn the body to the left, and stand on the right leg, slightly bent. Move the left leg backward and upward to below the buttocks. Continue to move the left arm to the left and back upward to draw a small circle. Then bend the arm and move it to the front of the right shoulder, palm centre down. Raise the right arm obliquely behind, and bend the trunk forward. Eyes front (Fig. 4-63).

4. Shift the body weight backward, press the right foot forcefully and skip half a step backward. Land the left foot obliquely behind, ball on the ground, both legs slightly bent, and bend the trunk forward (Fig. 2-117).

5. Bend the trunk horizontally to the left. Shift the body weight to the left leg. After pressing the ground, move the right leg swiftly to arc up backward, instep flat. At the same time, swing both arms horizontally to the left. Eyes front (Figs. 2-118, 119).

6. Continue to bend the trunk horizontally and turn it to the left backward. After pressing the ground, swing the left leg to the left upward. Continue to swing the right leg upward, and swing both arms to the left (Fig. 2-120).

7. Land the right foot and bend the knee as a buffer. Drop the left leg naturally (Fig. 4-64).

2) Technical Essentials

1. Make full use of the inertia from the three-step run and body turn to increase the power for jumping into the air. The first two steps should be quick and the skipping step a bit slower. Swinging of the arms should coordinate

with the turning of the trunk.

2. Before pressing the ground, relax and bend the trunk forward and twist and turn the body slightly to the right. This will increase the preparatory swing before the horizontal turn to the left.

3. Press the ground powerfully with the right foot first, and then the left foot, and swing the legs to the rear upward—apart and straight. Twist and turn the waist forcefully to the left backward. At the same time, swing both hands to the left powerfully, left hand before the right. Raise the head slightly while in the air.

4. Bend the knees in landing, naturally and lightly.

3) How to Practice

Execution of the butterfly movements calls for spring and power. It also requires pliability and coordination.

1. First do the exercises for backward leg stretch and backward kick, or bend the trunk forward, place the hands on an object and kick to the rear upward. At the same time, do the swallow balance exercise. Increase the standing time properly. Throughout these exercises, increase the kicking height of the backward swinging leg and improve the quality of the reverse bow pattern of the body in the air.

2. Bend both knees to half squat. Bend the trunk forward, swing it to the right, and then turn it to the left backward forcefully. Swing both arms horizontally and shift the body weight to the left. Bend the left knee and straighten the right, toes on the ground. As the body turns, keep the legs close to the ground and move them to behind the body (Figs. 2-152, 153). This exercise is intended for the practitioner to understand the turning power and speed of twisting the waist and swinging the arms, and coordination between the waist and the arms.

3. Do the exercises for swallow balance turning. The

Fig. 2-152

Fig. 2-153

start is the same as for the butterfly, but the left foot must not be off the ground. With the ball of the left foot as the axis, turn the body to the left and right by making use of the inertia from the swing of the waist and arms. This helps to increase the swinging power, and also the balancing ability (Fig. 2-154).

4. Place hands on a supporting object (not higher than waist level), and do the exercise for body turning with high leg-swinging. This is intended to increase the muscular power of the waist and back, and help acquire sufficient height for the backward leg swinging in the air.

5. Protection. The assistant stands by the left side of the practitioner, holds the left arm or wrist with the left hand, and places the right hand on the stomach of the practitioner. While the beginner executes the turning jump, the assistant holds up his body by the right hand. At the same time, he should use the left hand to draw the practitioner to the left backward and use the right hand to help turn the body (Figs 2-155, 156).

6. Practice the complete butterfly movement.

4) Common Mistakes and Corrections

1. Rising too early and raising the head too much.

Practise the movements in Figs. 2-152, 153, and put stress on bending the trunk forward horizontally. Do more protection exercises to effectively control the trunk and increase the height of the backward swinging leg.

2. Head down, waist arched and legs bent.

The main cause is insufficient pliability of the waist and legs. Practise more in the backward leg kick movements, and standing and turning swallow balance. In the course of practice, keep the chest out, head up, waist dropped, stomach extended, knees straight and insteps flat.

3. The turning movement is small and slow.

Apart from doing the exercise in No. 2, ask an assistant

Fig. 2-154

Fig. 2-155

Fig. 2-156

to assist you to solve the problem.

Jumping Front Kick

Jumping is one of the principal techniques in Wushu. Jumping exercises are indispensable to increase the springing ability of the legs and improve their quality. There are many jumping movements, divided into four groups: (1) straight body jumping, including jumping front kick, consecutive jumping front kick, jumping cross kick and jumping snap kick; (2) body turning jumping kick, including jumping and spinning lotus kick, body turning slap kick; (3) butterfly jumping kick, including whirlwind kick and butterfly, and (4) leaping, such as forward giant leaping. At present, the common jumping movements in the Wushu routines include: jumping front kick, spinning lotus kick, whirlwind kick, butterfly and giant leaping. Following is a description of the jumping front kick:

1) Description

Please do the exercises as described from Fig. 2-97 through Fig. 2-103. There are two landing postures: (1) rise and land with the left leg first. (2) jump up with the left leg and withdraw it to the front of the body. Slap quickly and land with the right leg. The first choice is for the beginners; the second requires good spring, a certain jumping height and quick snap of the right leg.

2) How to Practice

Jumping front kick not only calls for good spring and explosive force, but also for a certain pliability so as to complete the movement of slapping the feet in the air. Therefore, some exercises should be done to improve the quality of the movements so as to lay a good foundation for grasping the complete exercise.

1. Leg stretch and kick

Jumping front kick is a slapping kick, but it is executed

on the basis of the straight leg kick. First, do some exercises such as front leg stretch, high leg stretch and front kick to improve the pliability of the legs and the nimbleness of the joints. This will result in a kick start that is quick and natural. It can also help to avoid the spraining of ligaments and muscles while performing the fast and violent movements.

2. Front slap kick

Learn to do the exercises for the front slap kick on the basis of leg stretch and kick, in order to further improve the pliability of the legs and the accuracy of slapping between the hand and foot. It should be noted that the upward moving leg is straight, with instep flat. The palm is used to slap the front part of the instep. The slap should be accurate, loud, and clear.

3. Jumping

The height of the jumping movements depends, in a large degree, on the correctness of the starting movement. Before learning the movements, it is essential to repeatedly practise the start in order to obtain the best starting angle. You need to understand the coordination between the other body parts and the right foot at the moment of stepping. There are two starting methods: (1) Start by withdrawing the left foot (Fig. 2-157). The number of running steps is not limited. However, after the start, when the right foot steps forward, you should land the heel on the ground first, and stretch the leg forward, hips slightly forward. While shifting the body weight, you should land the right foot firmly, knee slightly bent, and then quickly kick the ground and jump up, left knee naturally raised and arms swinging upward. The main purpose is to understand the coordination between the heel kicking, waist lifting and arms swinging. (2) Start with running and a slap. During the practice, attention should be focused on the running speed. The last two steps, especially, should be quick. Only when the run is fast and the start is correct can you obtain the ideal jumping height.

4. Complete movement exercises

Jumping front kick is a difficult jumping movement. Therefore, it takes some time to learn it, and it is wise not to act with undue haste. A beginner should not overstress the jumping height and the landing of the right foot. First learn to land the left foot. When you have acquired some foundation and jumping height, proceed to learn how to land the right foot.

After the jumping height rises, the intervening time between the clapping and the foot slapping movement in the air should be shortened as much as possible. Attention should also be paid to the pattern formed in the air at that very moment.

5. Increase explosive force and spring

After grasping the movements and skills, you must have strong explosive force and spring, so as to acquire an ideal jumping height. You can practise in many ways. You can either do the exercises barehandedly or with equipment. They include standing jumping, upward jumping with legs bent, jumping from steps, half-squat jumping, rope skipping and heels rising and falling.

6. Training of waist, stomach and back muscles

Apart from the exercises described above, training of the waist, stomach and back muscles to increase their power should not be neglected. When this power is increased, it will help to increase the take-off speed of the legs and the controlling ability of the left leg after the slap.

Raise both ends of the body (Fig. 2-158). The practitioner is required to lie flat on the ground and then raise the trunk and feet at the same time and get them close together. Use both hands to slap the insteps. Continue to do this exercise repeatedly at a quick rate. Or lie on the stomach and raise the legs, hands and trunk upward to the utmost extent (Fig. 2-159). There are many ways, but I have described only two of them.

3) Common Mistakes and Corrections

1. Failure to slap the right foot

The causes for failure are insufficient pliability and increased difficulty in the leg technique after jumping. The third cause is the lack of proficiency in grasping the skills. Practise more in executing the front slap kick and lower the jumping height.

2. The right leg is bent while slapping

Consciously correct this mistake during practice and continue to do the exercises that help to improve the pliability of the legs.

3. The forward run is too far for a higher jump

The beginner often strides forward instead of jumping due to the wrong take-off angle and improper use of power. Practise more in executing the movements described in Fig. 2-157 to gradually acquire a correct pattern of motive force for the jumping take-off. Only in this way is it possible to constantly improve the quality of the movement and increase the jumping height.

4. Bending the trunk too far forward and sitting on the hips after the take-off with the result that the body weight drops. Practise more in executing the front slap kick. Keep the body straight and the hips forward. While executing the complete movement, grasp the correct way of forming the patterns and properly lower the jumping height to overcome the mistake.

4) Points for Attention

1. Choice for proper place

There should be a proper place for doing the exercises. They can be performed in a field, a lawn or on a carpeted

Fig. 2-157   Fig. 2-158

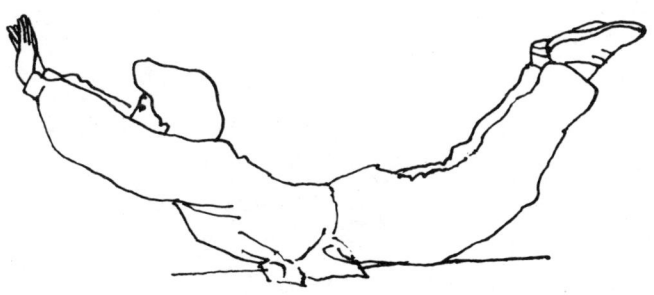

Fig. 2-159

floor. Uneven ground, slippery ground or ground with water are not suitable for running and jumping exercises. Also, it is advisable not to perform the exercises on a cement floor, because it is too hard and can easily injure the knee joints in jumping. It might cause ankle sprain and inflammation of the shin bone.

2. Warm-ups

Warm-ups are needed to excite the central nervous system so that the functions of the internal organs can gradually suit the needs of the movements to avoid injuries. Run slowly, do bare-handed exercises or play games to warm up the body parts before practice.

Chapter Three
Combinations

Routine exercises are basic technique exercises, composed of the basic movements in Chinese boxing, with or without weapons, in combination with the required hand, eye, body and foot techniques. The principle of proceeding from the easy to the difficult and from the simple to the complicated should be followed in practising the routine exercises. Generally speaking, three to six movements are preferred at the beginning. Through the routine exercises, one can improve the coordinating ability of the body and grasp the essentials of connecting the movements. They are the basis of the routines and are the basis for learning more difficult movements.

Particular attention has been paid to the composition of the routines. For example, stress is laid on the stances, leg techniques, balances and jumping. This helps to improve the skills quickly. In short, apart from grasping the norms for the stances, hand techniques, leg techniques, balances and jumping movements, you should also pay attention to the coordination among the eyes, hands, body, feet and stances. That is, the eyes should follow the hands, the body turns with the footwork and the footwork changes with the stances. Attention should also be paid to the positions for the advance and retreat of the feet. The steps should be proper for the connecting movements and changes. All this is in technical preparation for practising complete routine exercises.

Following is a description of a routine mainly composed of leg techniques for beginners:

Side sole kick—inside kick with body turn—push palm with bow step, and hooked hand—prostrate backward leg sweep—front kick with body turnback—palm chopping with bow step.

1. Starting Position

Stand with feet together, arms naturally down (Fig. 2-129).

2. Side Sole Kick

(1) Cross the hands in front of the body, the right outside, arms slightly bent. Then move them downward, forward, and upward in a curve to above the head, palm centre forward. Eyes front (Fig. 3-1).

(2) Shift the body weight to the left, skip the right foot obliquely forward over the left foot, toes outward, legs bent to a cross, left heel off the ground. When the palms drop down by the sides of the body, move them further downward and upward in a curve and cross them in front of the body. Snap the wrists to form upright palms in front of the chest. Turn the head to the left when snapping the wrists. Eyes left front (Fig. 3-2).

(3) Stand firmly on the right leg, bend the left leg and raise it to the left and kick forward to the upper left. Push the palms to both sides respectively, lean the trunk obliquely to the right side. Eyes on the left palm (Fig. 3-3).

Essentials: In executing the side sole kick, first bend and then extend the legs, straighten the knees, open the hips and kick fiercely with the power on the heel. Refrain from bending the trunk forward.

3. Inside Kick with Body Turn

(1) Shift the body weight to the left, left foot down, toes outward, both legs slightly bent. Raise the right arm by the

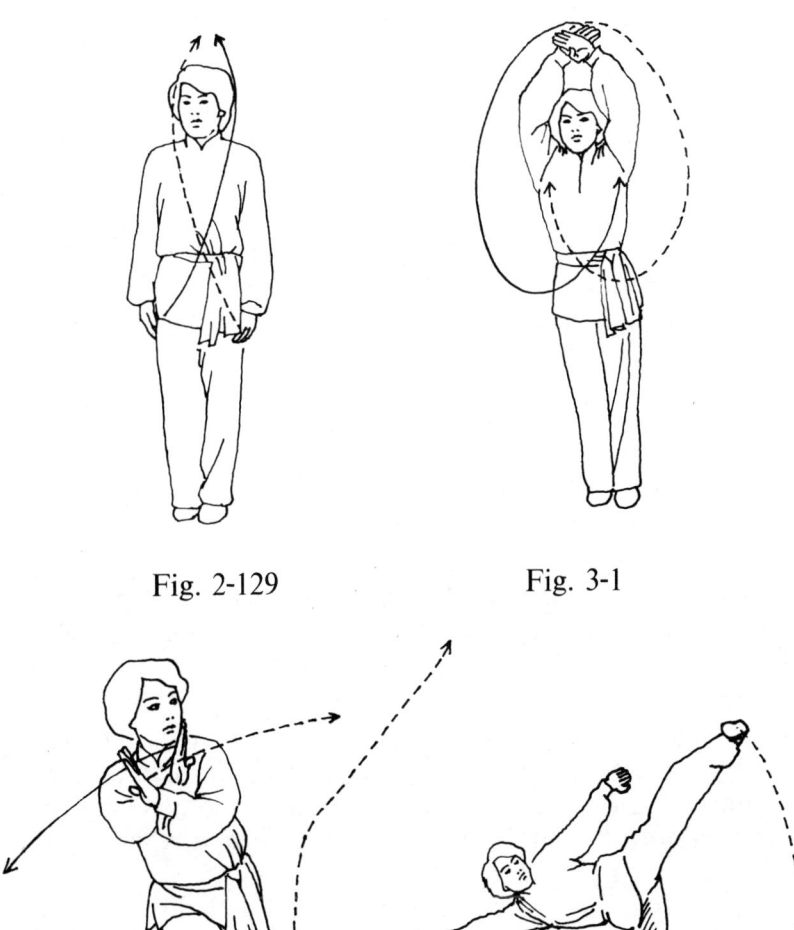

Fig. 2-129

Fig. 3-1

Fig. 3-2

Fig. 3-3

body side, move the left palm obliquely upward, thumb down. Eyes on the left palm (Fig. 3-4).

(2) Shift the body weight to the left leg, turn the body to the left, move the right leg upward from the right and swing it with a kick to the left, toes turned upward and inward. Slap the right sole with the left palm in front of the head to the left. Swing the right arm naturally to the body side together with the turning of the body. Eyes on the left palm (Figs. 3-5A, 5B).

Essentials: In executing the inside kick, swing the leg first to the right upward and then to the left in the fan shape. The slap should be quick and accurate.

4. Palm Pushing with Bow Step and Hook Hand

(1) Bend the left leg at the knee to support the body, and continue to turn the body to the left. Bend the right leg and withdraw it to the inner side of the left leg. Swing the left arm horizontally forward, and bend the right arm at the knee. Withdraw it to the waist, palm face up (Fig. 3-6).

(2) Bend the left leg at the knee to a squat, move the right leg obliquely backward, and straighten the knee to form a left bow step. Turn the right palm into an upright palm and push it forward quickly. Continue to swing the left palm to the left and backward to form a reverse arm hook hand. Eyes front (Fig. 3-7).

Essentials: While bending the left leg, land the right foot. The bow step, push palm and hook hand should be well-coordinated and shoulders relaxed. Drop the hips and avoid thrusting the buttocks out.

5. Prostrate Backward Sweep

(1) Raise the body weight slightly, turn the trunk slightly to the left and swing the arms naturally forward. Eyes

Fig. 3-4

Fig. 3-5A

Fig. 3-5B

front (Fig. 3-8).

(2) Bend the left leg to full squat, heel slightly off, and straighten the right leg to form a right crouch step. Bend the trunk forward and turn it to the right, both hands on the ground under the right leg (Fig. 3-9).

(3) With the left ball as the axis, continue to turn the body backward to the right, and sweep around 360 degrees, leg straight and right sole on the ground. Eyes obliquely down (Fig. 3-10).

Essentials: straighten the right leg and keep the heel on the ground. Bend the left leg to full squat in the course of the sweep. Drop the buttocks to lower the body weight. Twist the trunk to the right backward as much as possible to increase the sweeping speed.

6. Front Kick with Turn-back Body

(1) Shift the body weight backward to an upright position, right leg slightly bent and left leg straight. At the same time, swing the right arm upward and forward

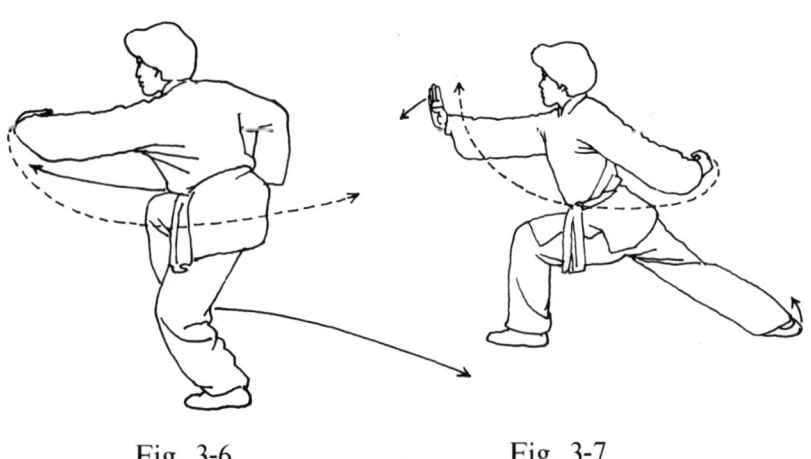

Fig. 3-6   Fig. 3-7

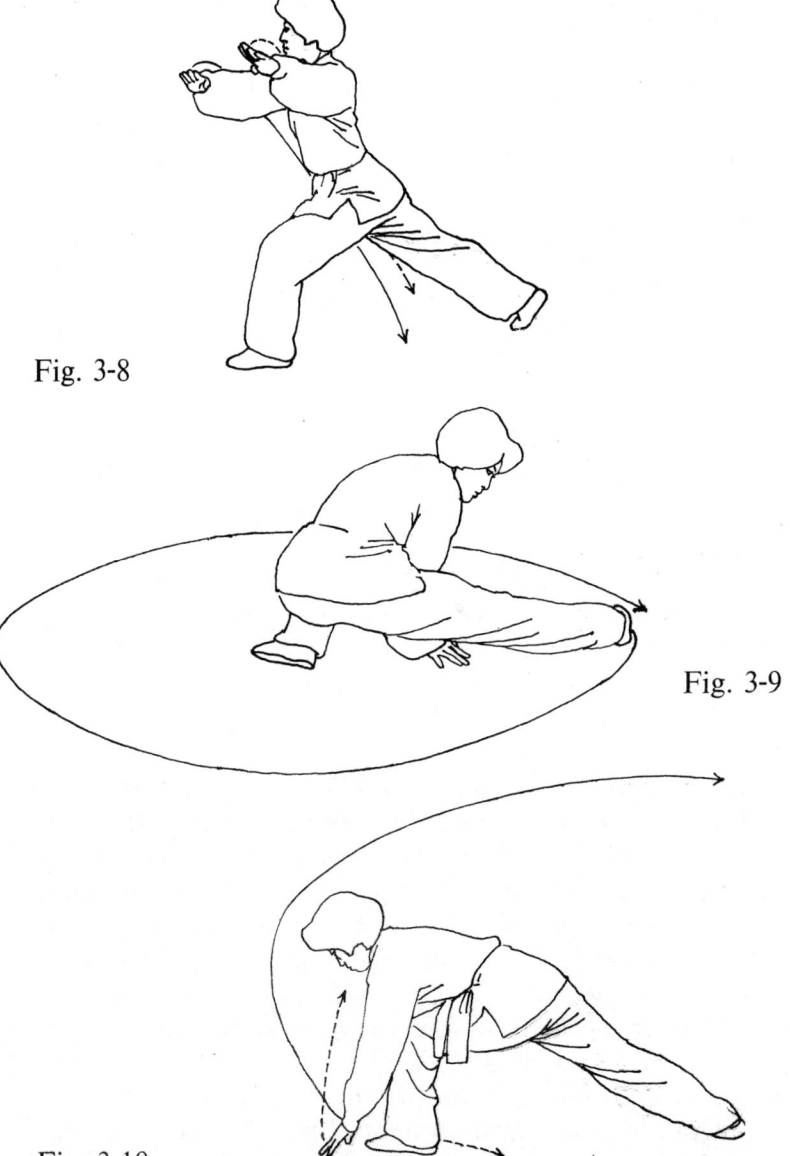

Fig. 3-8

Fig. 3-9

Fig. 3-10

together with the turning of the body. Swing the left arm upward. Eyes right front (Fig. 3-11).

(2) Continue to turn the trunk to the right, both legs slightly bent. Swing the right arm downward and backward, and the left arm upward and forward. Eyes front (Fig. 3-12).

(3) Shift the body weight forward, stand on the right leg for support, and kick with the left leg upward quickly, toes hooked. Swing the right palm forward and upward and flash it above the head to the right. Hook the left hand and swing it downward and backward. Eyes front (Fig. 3-13).

Essentials: Arm swinging should be continuous, and kicking of the left leg should be quick. Keep the legs straight, waist erect and head upright.

7. Palm Chopping with Bow Step

(1) Move the left foot forward, toes outward, both legs slightly bent and right heel off the ground. Swing the right arm forward, turn the left hook hand into palm and raise it obliquely backward, both arms straight. Eyes front (Fig. 3-14).

(2) Shift the body weight forward. Stand on the left leg for support. Bend the right leg and raise it forward, right foot close to the back of the left leg. Raise the left arm upward and continue to swing the right arm downward, past the left chest and upward. Slap the back of the right palm with the left palm above the head. Eyes front (Fig. 3-15).

(3) Shift the body weight forward, step with the right foot forward and bend the knee to form a right bow step. Chop from above downward with the right palm to the front of the body, arm straight. Drop the left palm and withdraw it to the side of the waist, palm centre up. Bend

Fig. 3-11   Fig. 3-12

Fig. 3-13

Fig. 3-14

Fig. 3-15   Fig. 3-16

the trunk forward slightly. Eyes on the right palm (Fig. 3-16).

Essentials: Shift the body weight forward before forming the bow step, and land the right foot simultaneously with the chopping. The movement should be quick and clean.

Chapter Four
Basic Routines

1. Names

First Part
1. Starting Form
2. Hold Fists with Feet Together
3. Flash Palm with Forward Toe Step
4. Thrust Fist with Left Bow Step
5. Punch with Heel Kick
6. Thrust Fist with Right Bow Step
7. Press Palm with Stamp and Punch Fist with Bow Step
8. Push Palm with Raised Knee
9. Giant Leap Forward
10. Push Palm with Bow Step and Hook Hand
11. Front Slap Kick
12. Elbow Forward with Bow Step
Second Part
13. Swing up Fist with Bow Step
14. Upper Block and Fist Chop with Horse-Riding Step
15. Thread Palm with Raised Knee
16. Thread Palm with Crouch Step
17. Jumping Front Kick with Forward Step
18. Palm Chop with Bow Step
19. Flash Palm with Crouch Step and Hooked Hand
20. Palm Slap with Crouch Step and Arm Swing
21. Punch Fist with Seated Step
Third Part
22. Sweep Side Punch with Bow Step

23. Backward Leg Sweep with Hands on Ground
24. Hammer Strike with Feet Together and Stamp
25. Front Kick with Forward Step
26. Swing Palms with Cross Step
27. Turn Waist Over
28. Fist Chop with Bow Step
29. Upper Block and Punch with Crossed Legs
Fourth Part
30. Butterfly with Skipping Step
31. Front Slap Kick
32. Close-to-Body Palm
33. Swing up Palm with Bow Step
34. Upper Block and Punch with Empty Step
35. Press Palm with Feet Together
36. Finishing Form

2. Descriptions

First Part

1. Starting Form

Stand with feet together, arms down by both sides and fingers together against the outer sides of the legs. Eyes front (Fig. 2-129).

Essentials: Keep the head upright, the chest out, the waist erect and the stomach in, arms slightly bent and naturally down.

2. Hold Fists with Feet Together

Stand on both legs, hands clenched into fists and withdrawn to the waist side, fist centre up. Turn the head to the left. Eyes left front (Fig. 2-130).

Essentials: Keep both fists tightly against the waist side, elbow joints backward and pressed inward. Relax the shoulders and pull the stomach in.

3. Flash Palm with Forward Toe Step

(1) Move the right foot obliquely forward to the right,

leg slightly bent and left leg straight. Turn the left fist into a palm and thrust it forward obliquely above, arm straight. Turn the arm outward, palm up, and keep the right fist on the hip. Eyes on the left palm (Fig. 4-1).

(2) Straighten the right leg, and kick the left shank forward quickly, toes on the ground. At the same time, turn the right fist into a palm, thread it forward over the left palm, turn the wrist over and flash it over the head to the left. Bend the left arm at the elbow and drop it down. Turn the left palm into a fist after threading and withdraw it to the waist side, fist centre up. Eyes left front (Fig. 4-2).

Essentials: Forward toe step and palm flash should be completed at the same time. Shift the body weight slightly to the right leg in forming the forward toe step. Thrust the chest out and pull the stomach in.

4. Thrust Fist with Left Bow Step

(1) Bend the right leg at knee, move the left foot to the

Fig. 2-130

Fig. 4-1

left side, toes turned outward into a half-horse step. At the same time, move the left fist forward and to the left in a curve for a parry, and keep the right fist by the waist side. Eyes left front (Fig. 2-131).

(2) Straighten the right leg forcefully and bend the left leg at knee to form a left bow step. At the same time, turn the body to the left, and thrust the right fist forward quickly, fist to the shoulder level. Bend the left arm at elbow and withdraw the fist to the waist side, fist centre up. Eyes on the right fist (Fig. 2-132).

Essentials: Turn the waist and extend the shoulders while punching. Keep the rear foot on the ground in forming the bow step.

5. Punch with Heel Kick

Shift the body weight forward and stand upright on the left leg. Bend the right leg at knee, raise it and kick forward forcefully, leg straight and foot hooked. At the same time, thrust the left fist forward, and withdraw the right fist to the waist side. Eyes left (Fig. 4-3).

Essentials: Stand firmly on the left leg and kick with power on the heel. Pull the right hip in and extend the left shoulder.

6. Thrust Fist with Right Bow Step

Lower the body weight, bend the left leg at knee and drop the right leg down, heel first and then whole foot on the ground. Straighten the left leg forcefully and bend the right leg at knee into a right bow step. At the same time, turn the trunk to the left, thrust the right fist forward to the right and withdraw the left fist to the waist side, elbow bent, and palm up. Eyes on the right fist (Fig. 4-4).

Essentials: Land the right foot before turning the trunk to the left and punching the fist. Make use of the power from the turning of the trunk to thrust the right fist with force to the fist centre.

Fig. 2-132

Fig. 4-2   Fig. 4-3

7. Press Palm with Stamp and Punch Fist with Bow Step

(1) Shift the body weight to the left leg, slip the right foot backward, front sole on the ground, and bend both legs at knee. Turn the right fist into palm, and the arm inward, elbow slightly bent, and chop it down in front of the body, thumb down. Turn the left fist into palm, and swing it forward to the inner side of the right arm, fingers up. Eyes on the right hand (Fig. 4-5).

(2) Press the right foot entirely on the ground. Swing the right arm downward, to the left, upward and to the right in a vertical circle. Swing the left arm to the left side of the body, both arms straight. Eyes right front (Fig. 4-6).

(3) Shift the body weight to the left, stand upright on the left leg and turn the body to the right with the front sole as the axis. Bend the right leg at knee and raise it up. At the same time, swing the right arm downward and the left arm upward. Eyes obliquely down (Fig. 4-7).

(4) Continue to turn the body to the right. Move the right foot to replace the left foot and stamp it. At the same time, raise the left foot and land it to the forward left, toes outward and legs slightly bent. Press the left palm downward in front of the body, palm down. Turn the right palm into fist, bend the elbow and withdraw it to the waist side. Eyes on the left hand (Fig. 4-8).

(5) Straighten the right leg and bend the left leg at the knee to form a left bow step. At the same time, turn the body to the left, thrust the right fist forward quickly, and bend the left elbow. Withdraw the left hand to under the right armpit, palm down. Eyes front (Fig. 4-9).

Essentials: While swinging the arm to press the palm, turn the waist to the left and right. Keep the arms close to the body and swing the arms in vertical circles. When stamping the right foot to change the step and turn the body, do not jump too high. There is no pause after

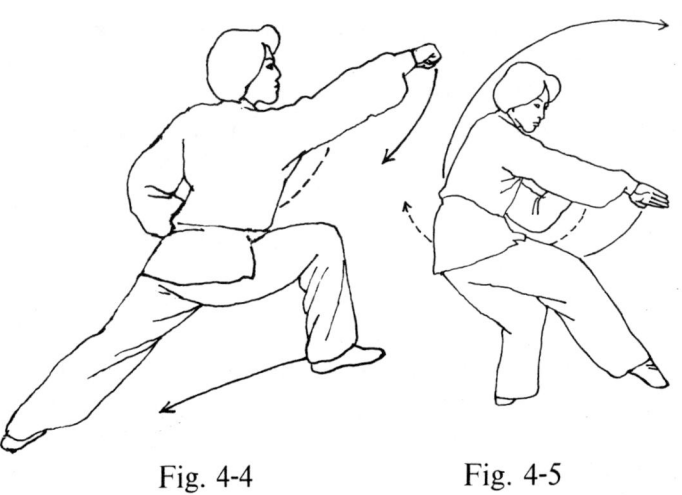

Fig. 4-4   Fig. 4-5

Fig. 4-6   Fig. 4-7

Fig. 4-8

Fig. 4-9

stamping the foot and pressing the palm, so go on immediately to thrust the fist with bow step.

8. Push Palm with Raised Knee

Shift the body weight to the right leg and stand upright on it. Bend the left leg at the knee and raise it up. At the same time, turn the trunk to the left, bend the right elbow and withdraw the right fist to the waist side. Push the left palm forward to the front left. Lean the trunk forward to the left. Eyes on the left hand (Fig. 4-10).

Essentials: Straighten the left leg before shifting the body weight, and then push the palm. Keep the left shank obliquely down and inward, instep flat.

9. Giant Leap Forward

(1) Land the left foot to the left, toes slightly outward. Step forward with the right foot, heel off the ground, legs slightly bent. Turn the trunk to the left, and swing the right arm upward, forward and downward, and the left arm downward and backward at the same time, body weight forward. Eyes front (Fig. 4-11).

(2) Press the ground with the left foot forcefully, bend the right leg at knee and raise it up. At the same time, swing the right arm forward and upward, and the left arm downward and upward while turning it outward, palm up. Eyes front (Fig. 4-12).

(3) In the air, swing the left shank up backward quickly and bend the right leg at the knee to stride forward. Turn the trunk backward and swing the left palm upward to the left above the head. Swing the right arm to the right at the shoulder level. Eyes on the right hand (Fig. 4-13).

(4) Land the right foot and bend the knee to full squat. Place the left foot in the front and straighten the leg to form a crouch step. At the same time, bend the right elbow and withdraw the palm to the waist side. Drop the left palm in a curve and press it in front of the right chest,

Fig. 4-10

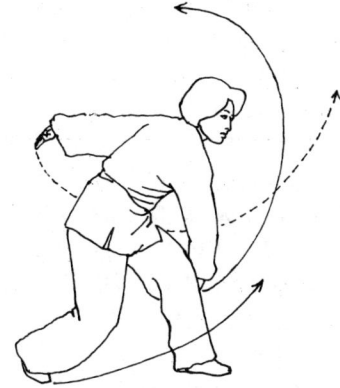

Fig. 4-11

Fig. 4-12

Fig. 4-13

fingers up. Eyes left front (Fig. 4-14).

Essentials: Both arms should coordinate with the left leg in pressing the ground. In the air, thrust the chest out, extend the stomach and swing the left leg to the rear upward. In landing to form a crouch step, slip the left foot forward on the ground.

10. Push Palm with Bow Step and Hook Hand

Bend the trunk forward to the side. Brush the left palm forward with thumb and forefinger down, to the left and downward above the left instep, arm straight.

Straighten the right leg and bend the left leg to form a left bow step. Turn the right palm into an upright palm and push it forward. Continue to swing the left palm backward and turn it into a reverse arm hook hand to the left behind the body, hook point up. Eyes front (Fig. 4-15).

Essentials: Brush the hand close to the left instep. While stepping forward with the right leg, keep the hips lowered and avoid raising the buttocks. Straighten both arms, turn the waist and drop the shoulders.

11. Front Slap Kick

(1) Shift the body weight backward, and move the left foot half a step backward, ball on the ground. Swing the right arm and raise it above the head to the right. Turn the left hook hand into a palm and swing it to the left and forward in a curve. Bend the elbow and withdraw the palm to the front of the right chest. Turn the trunk slightly to the left. Eyes front (Fig. 4-16).

(2) Shift the body weight to the left leg, swing the left arm downward and forward, and drop the right arm downward to behind the body, both arms straight. Eyes front (Fig. 4-17).

(3) Turn the body to the left, step forward with the right leg, heel off the ground. Raise the left arm up and swing the right arm downward, forward and upward, to slap the

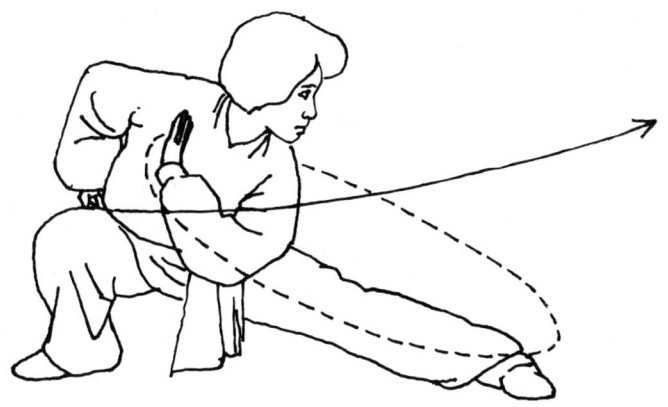

Fig. 4-14

Fig. 4-15　　　　Fig. 4-16

left palm centre with the right palm back. Eyes front (Fig. 4-18).

(4) Stand upright on the left leg, swing the right leg forward with a kick, instep flat. Move the right palm forward to slap the right instep. Raise the left arm obliquely upward to the body side. Eyes on the right hand (Fig. 4-19).

Essentials: Straighten the legs, keep the trunk from bending and thrust the hips forward. Slap the instep quickly, accurately and loudly.

12. Elbow Forward with Bow Step

(1) Stand upright on the left leg, land the right leg and bend the knee, right foot against the inner side of the left leg. Turn the right palm into a fist, bend the elbow and withdraw it to the front of the chest, fist centre down. Drop the left palm and bend the elbow, palm face against

Fig. 4-17

Fig. 4-18

the right fist centre, body weight forward. Eyes obliquely rear (Fig. 4-20).

(2) Step with the right foot forward, bend the knee to half squat, and straighten the left leg to form a right bow step. At the same time, push the elbow forward forcefully with the right elbow to the shoulder level. Eyes front (Fig. 4-21).

Essentials: While elbowing, keep the left palm tightly against the right fist and push them forward quickly. Push the elbow forward horizontally with power on the joint. Elbowing and forming of the bow step should be completed at the same time.

Second Part

13. Swing up Fist with Bow Step

Turn the body to the left, bend the left leg at the knee, and straighten the right leg to form a left bow step. Swing

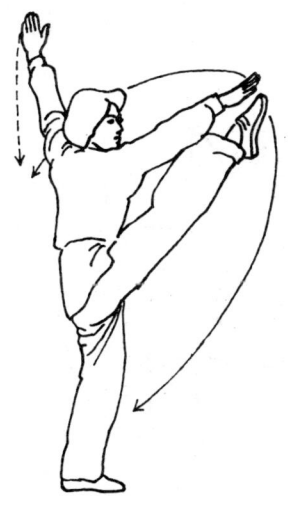

Fig. 4-19

Fig. 4-20

the right fist, arm straight, from right downward and forward, fist eye up. Swing the left palm forward, arm straight, together with the turning of the body, and then bend the elbow and withdraw it above the right forearm, palm down. Eyes on the right fist (Fig. 4-22).

Essentials: Turn the body at the same time you straighten the leg and turn the hips. The movements should be a bit slower, but there is no pause between two movements.

14. Upper Block and Fist Chop with Horse-Riding Step

Turn the upper part of the body and the feet to the right, with the balls on the ground forcefully, to form a horse-riding step. At the same time, swing the right fist forward, upward and to the right and chop forcefully together with the turning of the body. Swing the left palm to the left and upward, flashing it to the left over the head. Eyes right front (Fig. 4-23).

Essentials: Fist chop with horse-riding step should be

Fig. 4-21

completed in continuity with the previous form, first slowly and then quickly. The turning of the body should be abrupt. Relax and lower the shoulders.

15. Thread Palm with Raised Knee

(1) Turn the body slightly to the right and move the right foot obliquely backward, ball on the ground, and legs slightly bent. At the same time, swing and press the left palm across the head to the front of the body, elbow slightly bent and palm centre down. Bend the right elbow and withdraw the fist to the waist side. Eyes on the left hand (Fig. 4-24).

(2) Shift the body weight backward and stand upright on the right leg. Bend the left leg at the knee and raise it, instep flat. While turning the right fist into palm, thread it forward over the back of the left hand. Turn the trunk slightly to the left and extend the right shoulder forward. Bend the left elbow and withdraw the palm to under the

Fig. 4-22   Fig. 4-23

right forearm, palm down. Eyes on the right hand (Fig. 4-25).

Essentials: Stand firmly with raised knee, extend the trunk slightly forward. The threading and pressing of the palms should be well-coordinated.

16. Thread Palm with Crouch Step

(1) Bend the right leg at knee to squat, land the left foot to the left side, toes inward, and straighten the leg to form a left crouch step. At the same time, thread the left palm from the chest to the left along the inner side of the left leg to above the instep. Raise the right arm obliquely upward to the right side. Lean the trunk forward to the left. Eyes on the left hand (Fig. 4-26).

(2) Straighten the right leg and bend the left leg at knee. Continue to thread the left palm forward and up, and raise the right arm by the body side. Eyes left front (Fig. 4-27).

Essentials: While squatting, bend the right leg and slip

Fig. 4-24   Fig. 4-25

the left foot forward. The threading of the left palm should be close to the body, both arms straight. There are no pauses between the movements.

17. Jumping Front Kick with Forward Step

(1) Turn the body to the left, move the right foot forward, and straighten the knee, heel on the ground. At the same time, swing the left arm upward and drop the right arm naturally. Eyes front (Fig. 4-28).

(2) Keep the whole right foot on the ground, press the ground forcefully to jump up, and swing the left leg to kick forward and upward. Put up the left arm and swing the right arm downward, forward and upward to slap the left palm with the back of the hand. Eyes front (Fig. 4-29).

(3) Bend the left leg at the knee in the air and withdraw it to the front of the body. Swing the right leg swiftly to kick forward above, instep flat. At the same time, move the right palm down to meet the right instep and lift the

Fig. 4-26   Fig. 4-27

left arm obliquely above, trunk slightly forward. Eyes on the right hand (Fig. 4-30).

Essentials: Continue immediately from the previous form. The take-off of the right foot should be quick, and the slapping should be continuous, accurate and loud.

18. Palm Chop with Bow Step

(1) Land the left foot, then move the right foot immediately forward, bending both legs as a buffer. Straighten the arms and raise them horizontally on both sides. Eyes front (Fig. 4-31).

(2) Turn the body to the left, straighten the right leg and bend the left leg to form a left bow step. At the same time, turn the right arm outward, palm up, and chop obliquely up to the right together with the turning of the body. Bend the left elbow and withdraw the palm to the waist side, palm up. Eyes on the right palm (Fig. 4-32).

Essentials: Leg straightening and palm chopping should be completed at the same time. Extend the right shoulder forward. In chopping, exert the force to the outer edge of the palm.

19. Flash Palm with Crouch Step and Hooked Hand

(1) Turn the right arm inward and bend the elbow to press downward. Thread the left palm forward above the back of the right hand. Eyes on the left palm (Fig. 4-33).

(2) Turn the body to the right, bend the right leg at the knee and straighten the left leg. Swing the right hand downward, and to the right backward in a circle. Raise the left arm to the side of the body, both arms straight, palm forward. Eyes on the right palm (Fig. 4-34).

(3) Bend the right leg to full squat, and straighten the left leg to form a left crouch step. Move the right hand upward in a curve, snap the wrist and flash the palm to the upper right above the head. At the same time, continue to brush and swing the left hand backward and form a

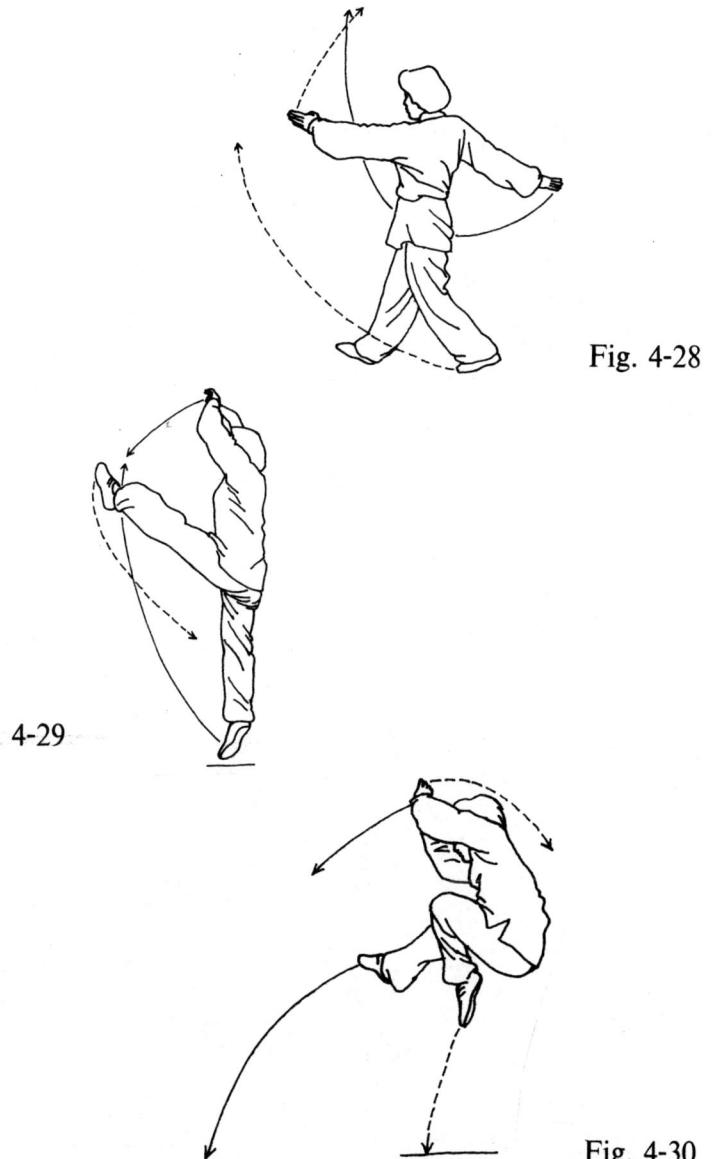

Fig. 4-28

Fig. 4-29

Fig. 4-30

Fig. 4-31   Fig. 4-32

Fig. 4-33   Fig. 4-34

reverse arm hook hand, tip up. Turn the head to the left. Eyes left front (Fig. 4-35).

Essentials: The complete movement should be closely connected, with no pause. The lower limbs should cooperate well in forming the crouch step, flashing the palm, forming the hook hand and turning the body.

20. Palm Slap with Crouch Step and Arm Swing

(1) Turn the trunk to the left, bend the left leg slightly and move the right leg forward and straighten it. Swing the right arm to the right, downward and forward, and swing the left arm to the rear, both arms straight. Eyes front (Fig. 4-36).

(2) Turn the trunk to the right, bend the right leg slightly and straighten the left leg. Swing the right arm upward and to the right, and the left arm downward and to the left at the same time. Eyes right front (Fig. 4-37).

(3) Continue to turn the trunk to the right. Swing the right arm downward and backward, with the left arm upward and forward at the same time, both arms straight. Eyes front (Fig. 4-38).

(4) Turn the trunk to the left, bend the left leg to full squat and straighten the right leg to form a right crouch step. At the same time, swing the right arm upward, to the right and downward, and slap the ground within the inner side of the right leg with the palm. Swing the left arm downward, to the left and upward and raise it to the upper left. Keep both arms straight. Eyes obliquely down (Fig. 4-39).

Essentials: The movements should be closely connected. In swinging the arms, turn the waist to both sides nimbly to keep both arms straight and close to the body. The movements should be quick. The crouch step and the slapping should be completed at the same time.

Fig. 4-35

Fig. 4-36

Fig. 4-37

21. Punch Fist with Seated Step

(1) Shift the body weight to the right, bend the right leg and move the left foot obliquely to behind the right foot, ball on the ground. At the same time, move the right hand from right upward and downward in a curve, pressing it to the left in front of the body. Turn the left palm into a fist, bend the elbow and withdraw it to the waist side, fist centre up. Eyes left front (Fig. 4-40).

(2) Bend the legs to full squat to form a seated step. At the same time, thrust the left fist to the left swiftly, turn the right palm into a fist and withdraw it to the waist side. Eyes on the left fist (Fig. 4-41).

Essentials: In moving the foot backward, the step should not be too big. In squatting, keep the legs close and firm, chest out and waist erect. Relax the shoulders.

Third Part

22. Sweeping Side Punch with Bow Step

(1) Move the left foot forward to the left, and bend the legs to half squat. Swing the right fist, arm straight,

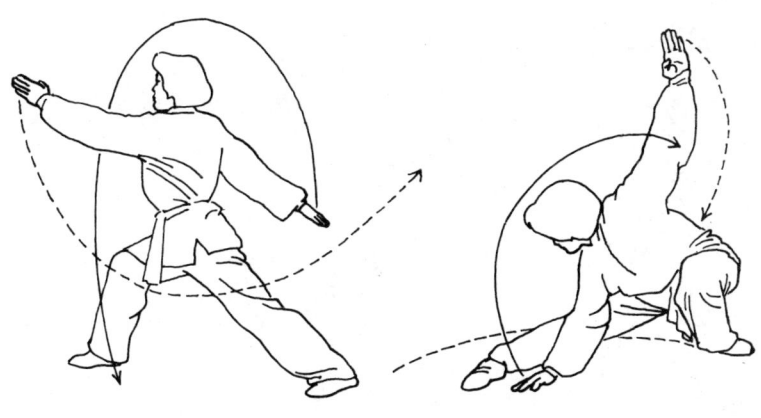

Fig. 4-38   Fig. 4-39

obliquely downward. Turn the left fist into palm and raise it forward to the left. Eyes on the right fist (Fig. 4-42).

(2) Shift the body weight forward to the left, straighten the right leg, and bend the left leg to a half squat to form a left bow step. Strike horizontally forward and to the left obliquely upward with the right fist. Slap the left palm with the fist over the head, both elbows slightly bent, trunk leaning to the left. Eyes on the left hand (Fig. 4-43).

Essentials: In the sweeping side punch, keep the fist eye obliquely down and exert force to the fist centre. Relax the shoulders and straighten the right leg in coordination with hip turning.

23. Backward Leg Sweep with Hands on Ground

(1) Bend the left leg at the knee to full squat, and stretch the right leg horizontally to form a right crouch step. Turn the trunk to the right backward and bend the body over the right leg, both palms on the ground under the right leg. Turn the left arm inward and the right arm outward and bend the wrist. Keep the fingers as backward as

Fig. 4-40   Fig. 4-41

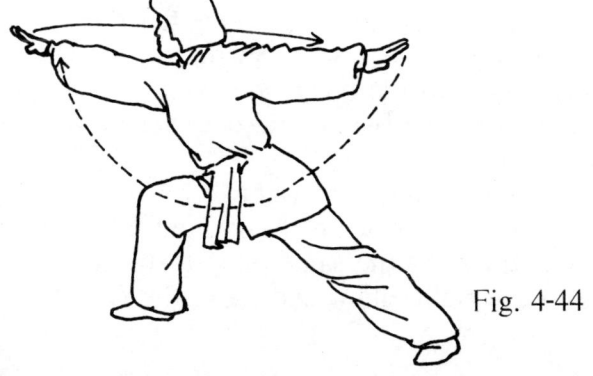

Fig. 4-42

Fig. 4-43

Fig. 4-44

possible. Eyes obliquely down (Fig. 2-44).

(2) With the ball of the left foot as axis, and hands on the ground, continue to turn the body to the right backward, and sweep around 360 degrees with the ball of the right foot on the ground. Eyes on the ground (Figs. 2-45, 46).

Essentials: In the course of the leg sweep, stretch the right leg backward and keep the heel on the ground. At the same time, lower the hips and avoid raising the buttocks.

24. Hammer Strike with Feet Together and Stamp

(1) Turn the trunk to the right, shift the body weight to the right leg, bend it to a half squat, and straighten the left leg. At the same time, swing the right arm horizontally to the right, and raise the left arm to the body side, both arms straight. Eyes right front (Fig. 4-44).

(2) Continue to turn the trunk to the right, swing the right arm horizontally to the right and backward, and the left arm downward and forward, both arms straight and left shoulder forward. Eyes front (Fig. 4-45).

(3) Continue to swing the left arm upward and turn the arm inward immediately with the palm up. Swing the right arm to obliquely downward. Keep the chest out and head upright. Eyes on the left hand (Fig. 4-46).

(4) Turn the trunk to the left, shift the body weight to the left leg and stand upright on the leg. Straighten the right leg, then bend the knee and raise it. Swing the left palm downward and press it to the body side, palm face down. Turn the right palm into a fist and raise it over the head. Eyes front (Fig. 4-47).

(5) Lower the body weight, move the right foot to the inner side of the left foot, stamp it on the ground, and bend both legs to half squat. At the same time, turn the left palm up and bend the right elbow and move the fist

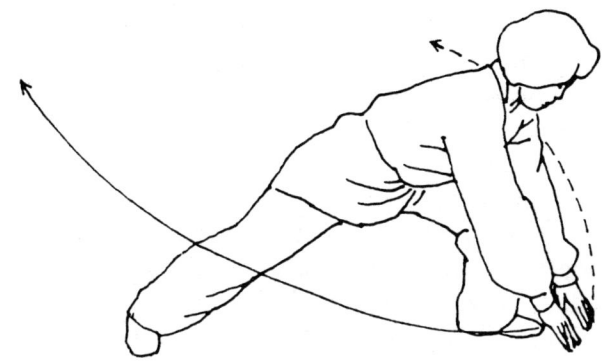

Fig. 2-46

Fig. 4-45　　　　　Fig. 4-46

down to hammer the left palm with the back of the hand. Eyes on the right fist (Fig. 4-48).

Essentials: In swinging the arms, turn the waist and extend the shoulders. The movements should be quick and closely connected. The stamping should be executed with the whole sole on the ground, and simultaneously with the fist hammering. In the half squat with feet together, keep the chest out, drop the waist and keep the trunk from bending forward and the buttocks from rising.

25. Front Kick with Forward Step

(1) Shift the body weight and move the left foot forward, leg slightly bent. Straighten the right leg, heel off the ground. At the same time, turn the right fist into a palm and stretch it forward above. Swing the left arm from below to behind the body, both arms straight. Eyes front (Fig. 4-49).

(2) Shift the body weight forward, stand upright on the left leg and kick upward with the right leg quickly, toes

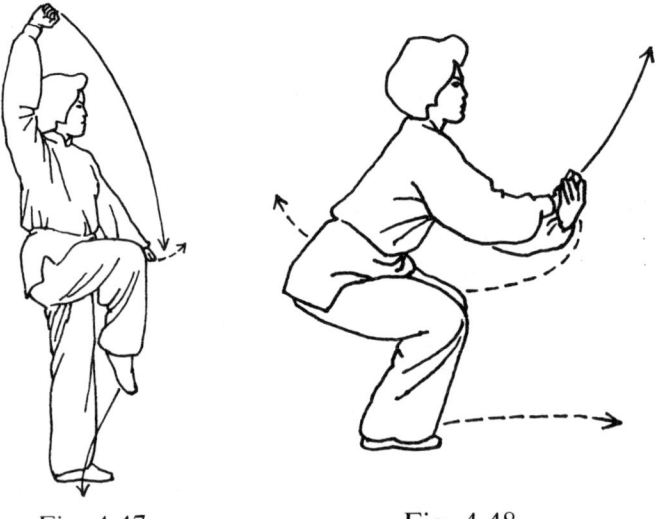

Fig. 4-47   Fig. 4-48

hooked. Swing the left palm forward and upward and flash it above the head to the left. Swing the right palm downward and backward and turn it into a hook, fingers up. Eyes front (Fig. 4-50).

Essentials: The kicking should be quick. Keep both legs straight and pull the buttocks in. Keep the trunk upright and keep from bending forward or backward.

26. Swing Palms with Cross Step

(1) Land the right foot forward, toes slightly inward, and leg slightly bent. Turn the right hook hand into palm and swing it from below and forward. Drop the left palm and withdraw it to the inner side of the right forearm, fingers of both hands forward. Eyes front (Fig. 4-51).

(2) Turn the body to the left, both legs slightly bent. Swing both arms downward and to the left, together with the turning of the body, right arm slightly bent at elbow.

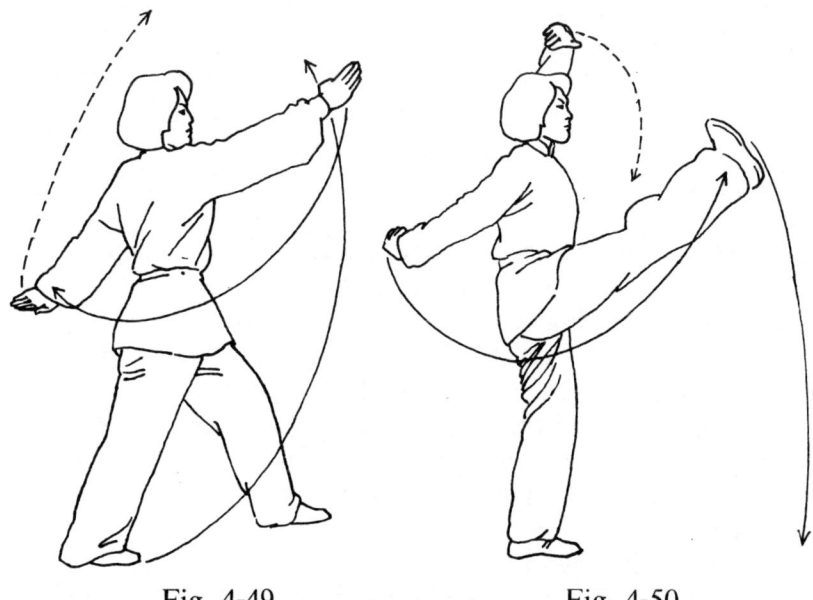

Fig. 4-49   Fig. 4-50

Eyes on the left hand (Fig. 4-52).

(3) Shift the body weight to the right leg and bend it to half squat, move the left foot to behind the right foot to form a back cross-step, ball on the ground, and leg straight. At the same time, swing both palms upward and to the right in curves, right arm straight. Bend the left elbow, and swing the palm to the front of the right shoulder, fingers of both palms up. Eyes on the right palm (Fig. 4-53).

Essentials: Relax the shoulders in swinging the palms. Palm swinging should be completed simultaneously with the back cross-step. Turn the trunk to the right and lower the hips.

27. Turn Waist Over

(1) Swing the left arm downward and to the left, and raise the right arm to the body side, fingers pointing sideways, thumbs and forefingers down. Bend the trunk forward. Eyes on the ground in front (Fig. 4-54).

(2) Turn the trunk to the upper left and bend it backward. With the balls as axis, turn feet, toes forward. Swing the right arm from below to the right and the left arm from above to the left, in curves at the same time. Eyes to the rear (Fig. 4-55).

(3) Continue to turn the trunk over, left toes immediately outward, right heel outward and raised, and both legs bent at knee. Swing the right arm from above to the right and the left arm from below to the left, at the same time in curves. Eyes right front (Fig. 4-56).

Essentials: Bend the trunk backward as much as possible. Keep the chest, stomach and hips out. Relax both shoulders. Straighten the arms and swing them quickly in vertical circles close to the body.

28. Fist Chop with Bow Step

(1) Shift the body weight to the left leg and stand

Fig. 4-51

Fig. 4-52

Fig. 4-53

upright on the leg. Bend the right leg and raise the knee, right foot against the inner side of the left shank. Lift the left arm and continue to swing the right arm downward and from the chest upward. Clap the left palm with the back of the right hand. Eyes front (Fig. 4-57).

(2) Shift the body weight forward to the right, land the right foot forward to the right and bend the knee to form a right bow step. Chop straight from above downward with the right fist with the fist eye upward. Turn the left palm into a fist, drop it, bend the elbow, and withdraw it to the waist side, fist centre up. Bend the trunk slightly forward to the right. Eyes on the right fist (Fig. 4-58).

Essentials: Shift the body weight before landing. Chopping should be quick and powerful. Relax both shoulders.

29. Upper Block and Punch with Crossed Legs

(1) Turn the body to the right, legs slightly bent. Turn the left fist into palm and swing it forward with the body turn, palm up. Bend the right elbow and withdraw the fist to the waist side. Eyes front (Fig. 4-59).

(2) Bend the right leg to half squat, bend the left leg at knee and hook the foot, toes tightly against the back of the right knee. Turn the trunk to the left, swing the left arm upward and block with the left palm over the head to the left. Punch the right fist forward to the right forcefully, fist eye up. Eyes on the right fist (Fig. 4-60).

Essentials: Stand firmly on the right leg, and keep the left foot against the right leg, forcing it forward slightly. Turn the waist and extend the shoulders in order to exert force for punching.

Fourth Part

30. Butterfly with Skipping Step

(1) Move the left foot to the left and shift the body weight to the left. Swing the right arm horizontally to the left, bend the left elbow and withdraw the left palm to

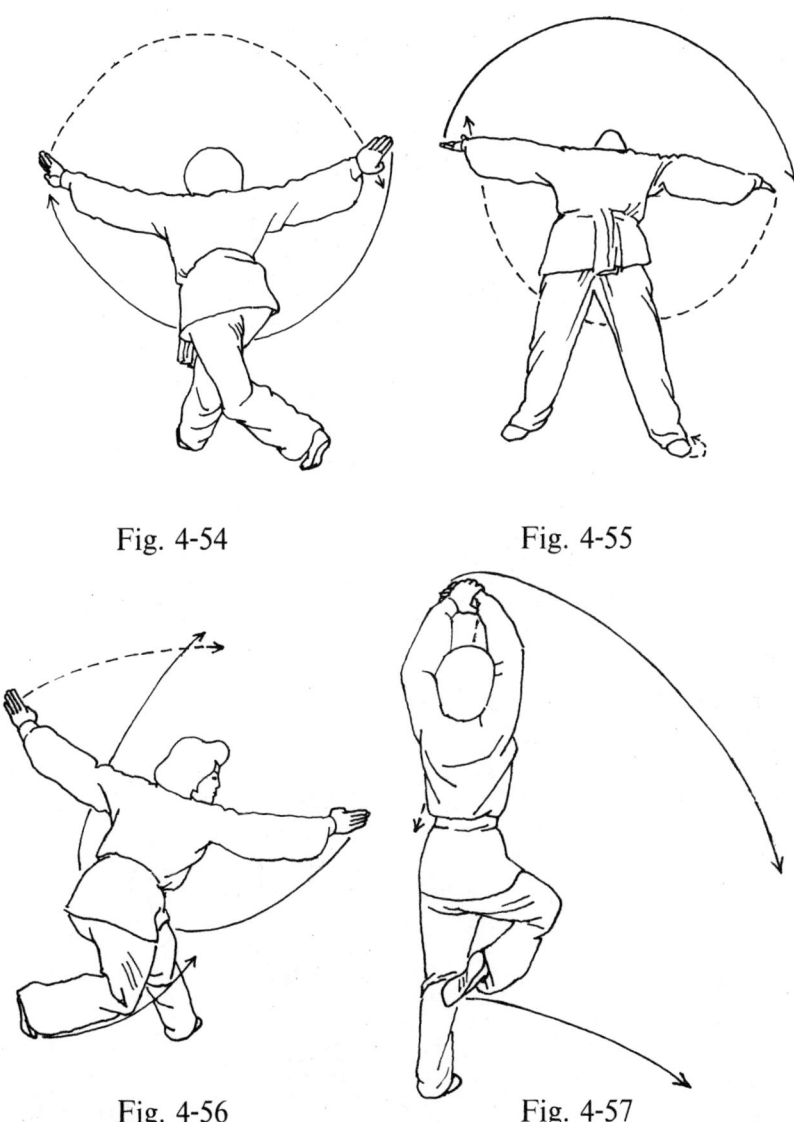

Fig. 4-54

Fig. 4-55

Fig. 4-56

Fig. 4-57

Fig. 4-58

Fig. 4-59

Fig. 4-60

under the right arm, both palms down. Eyes left front (Fig. 4-61).

(2) Turn the body slightly to the left, and move the right foot forward to the right, toes inward. Move the right arm immediately to the left, backward and to the right to draw a small circle over the head. At the same time, swing the left arm horizontally sideways. Keep both arms straight. Eyes right front (Fig. 4-62).

(3) Turn the body to the left and bend the right knee to support the body. Swing the left leg backward. Bend the left arm at elbow and withdraw the left palm to the front of the right shoulder, palm down, and right arm raised obliquely behind. Bend the trunk forward. Eyes front (Fig. 4-63).

(4) Shift the body weight backward and press the ground forcefully with the right leg. Skip half a step backward, left foot landing obliquely backward to the left, front sole on the ground, and both legs bent at knee (Fig. 2-117).

(5) Bend the trunk horizontally and turn it to the left, body weight shifted between the legs. Swing the arms horizontally sideways with the body turn (Fig. 2-118).

(6) Continue to bend the trunk horizontally and turn it to the left, body weight shifted to the left leg. Swing the right leg up quickly backward after stepping, instep flat. Swing both arms horizontally to the left at the same time. Eyes left forward (Fig. 2-119).

(7) Continue to twist and turn the trunk to the left and backward. Swing the left leg upward to the left after stepping, and the right leg upward to the right in a circle. Swing the arms horizontally to the left. Eyes left front (Fig. 2-120).

(8) Land the right foot on the ground, left leg immediately dropping behind the body. Swing the right arm to

Fig. 4-61

Fig. 4-62

Fig. 4-63

the front of the body, raise the left arm horizontally and obliquely behind, and bend the trunk forward slightly. Eyes front (Fig. 4-64).

Essentials: Make full use of the inertia from the body turn and skipping to increase the jumping power. Bend the trunk horizontally and turn it. Swing the right leg backward and upward first. Relax the arms and swing them to the left in coordination with waist twisting. Keep the chest out and the head up.

31. Front Slap Kick

(1) Turn the body to the left, right foot raised. Immediately kick the ground with the left foot and leap forward. Kick forward with the right foot to hit the left foot in the air. Raise the arms horizontally sideways. Eyes left front (Fig. 4-65).

(2) Land the right foot first, and put the left foot immediately forward, legs slightly bent. Raise both arms on the two sides (Fig. 4-66).

(3) Turn the body to the left, and shift the weight forward, right heel raised. Lift the left arm, swing the right arm downward, forward and upward, and slap the left palm with the back of the right hand over the head. Eyes front (Fig. 4-67).

(4) Stand upright on the left leg, swing the right leg forward to kick up, instep flat. Move the right palm to slap the right instep, left arm raised obliquely up sideward. Eyes on the right palm (Fig. 4-68).

Essentials: The same as described for Exercise 11.

32. Close-to-Body Palm

(1) Bend the left leg to full squat and the right leg at knee and put it down, ball on the ground and against the inner side of the left foot. Chop obliquely downward to the left with the right palm, bend the left arm at elbow and swing it downward. Withdraw the left palm to above the right arm. Eyes on the right palm (Fig. 4-69).

Fig. 2-120

Fig. 4-64

Fig. 4-65

Fig. 4-66

Fig. 4-67

Fig. 4-68

Fig. 4-69

(2) Move the right foot forward to the right, bend the knee to half squat, and straighten the left leg to form a right bow step. Swing the right palm obliquely upward and the left palm obliquely downward at the same time, arms straight. Eyes on the right palm (Fig. 4-70).

Essentials: Relax the shoulders, use the waist to drive the arms. Keep the chest in and back straight in chopping with the right palm. Straighten the arms when swinging the palms with bow step. Thrust the chest out and open the arms. Exert the force to the right shoulder and left arm.

33. Swing up Palm with Bow Step

Turn the body to the left, bend the left leg at knee and straighten the right leg to form a bow step. Swing the right palm immediately along the right side of the body downward and then swing it forward, arm straight. Withdraw the left palm to above the right arm, palm down. Eyes on the right palm (Fig. 4-71).

Essentials: Turn the waist and the hips and straighten the right leg when turning the body back to form the bow step. The movement should not be too quick. There should be no pause before continuing to do the next movement.

34. Upper Block and Punch with Empty Step

Shift the body weight backward. Bend the right leg to half squat, left toes on the ground, and slip it backward to form an empty step. Continue to swing the right arm forward, and upward, then turn the palm inward and turn the palm over for a block over the head to the right. At the same time, turn the left palm into a fist, withdraw it to the waist side and punch it obliquely forward quickly. Eyes on the left fist (Fig. 4-72).

Essentials: In order to exert force, the left fist should be withdrawn to the waist side before punching.

Fig. 4-70   Fig. 4-71

Fig. 4-72   Fig. 4-73   Fig. 4-74

35. Press Palm with Feet Together

(1) Shift the body weight to the right leg, put the left foot on the ground, leg straight. Swing the right arm forward, downward on the right side and obliquely upward in a curve. Turn the left fist into a palm and raise it obliquely downward to the body side. Keep both arms straight. Eyes on the right palm (Fig. 4-73).

(2) Shift the body weight to the left and move the right foot to the inner side of the left foot, legs straight. At the same time, swing both arms upward and then press them from the ears downward to the front of the hips, elbows slightly bent, palms down. Turn the head to the left. Eyes left front (Fig. 4-74).

Essentials: Keep the chest out and the stomach in, press the palms to the breadth of the shoulders and exert force to the heels of the palm.

36. Finishing Form

Keep both arms naturally down, thumb and fingers together against the outer sides of the legs. Eyes front (Fig. 2-129).

Chapter Five
How to Learn Long-Style Boxing Well

There is a correct way to learn long-style boxing *(Chang Quan)*. In the following paragraphs I'll make a few comments on how to learn it well and how to understand the basics.

1. Begin Slowly

The beginner should proceed step by step; that is, from the simple to the complicated and from the easy to the difficult.

You should start with the basics. By training in the basic skills, you will quickly and effectively improve the physical qualities needed by *Chang Quan* exercises. It will help you lay a good foundation for further improving the basic movements, difficult movements and routine performances. In learning the basics, you should decide how many times and how long to practise each movement, depending on your own physical condition. You should also pay attention to the coordinated development of your body by using the limbs alternately.

Through the training in the basic skills, your body will acquire the pliability, physical power and nimbleness required; you can then proceed to learn the basic movements. These are the elements that constitute the routines. The complete movements consist of hand forms, hand techniques, stances, footwork, such as balances, leg techniques, jumps and tumbling. Most of these movements are practised singly and repeatedly. You should understand the requirements for each movement through practice, and lay stress on the norms of the movements.

In the course of learning the basic movements and, after grasping the skills up to a certain stage, you should start to learn the routines. Because the dynamic patterns for the correct single movements are often formed in simple conditions, they do not reach the technical requirements of the diverse routines. Only by forming a new standard dynamic pattern for combination movements through combination exercises, will it be possible to improve the single movement technique. Apart from the combination exercises described above, you can also arrange your own combination exercises, each consisting of four to six movements.

Begin to learn the routines on the basis of what is described above. First, grasp four to five movements. After learning and performing them correctly, learn some more movements and then continue to learn and practise the complete routines. At the beginning, progress should be slow, especially while you are learning the inherent rhythms of *Chang Quan*. After practising for some time, and gradually grasping the rules, progress will become quicker.

In short, the process of learning requires progress in an orderly way, step by step, and according to one's capability. Do not be overanxious for success, nor aim too high. Otherwise, you will not only hinder learning, but also cause injuries.

2. Grasp the Correct Way of Movement

As a beginner, you should learn correct stances for the basic skills and movements. For example, in executing the front kick, it is possible that you may not touch the forehead with the toes at the beginning. If you insist on touching the forehead, you can bow your head or bend your body and knees. Therefore, you should first lower the kicking height and reduce the speed. It is good enough to kick a bit higher than the hips, but you should keep the neck upright, the chest out, the waist erect and the legs straight.

Then how do you grasp the correct method of movement?

1. Do exercises in a group. One person executes the movement, another describes the pictures and directions and a third person watches the exercises and prompts. Group exercises and discussions (three or more people) not only help increase interest in practice and correct your mistakes, but also deepen your impressions, accelerate your learning and put an end to the errors.

2. Separate the exercises; first do single movements and then combinations. For example, the snap kick and push palm exercise calls for straightening the supporting leg while kicking quickly with the other leg, and thrusting one fist forward while withdrawing the other to the waist side. But a beginner often finds this difficult. So you can first practice the kicking and punching separately. When you become skillful in the separate movements, you can then combine the separate movements into one exercise.

3. Combine practice with thinking. To grasp the correct way of doing exercises, you must first learn the correct concepts of the movements. If the concept is incorrect, there will be no correct movement. In doing the exercises, you should follow the order of "legs, body, hands and eyes." During the breaks, you can review the process of the movements and their requirements, so as to deepen the impression and correct the mistakes. After learning the movements, combinations and routines, you should also review the descriptions and points for attention stated in

the book. This is good for improving accuracy, consolidating what is learnt and deepening the understanding.

3. Intensify Physical Training

In executing the movements well, a beginner should also acquire good physical qualities (pliability, power, speed, spring, etc.). To acquire these qualities, you should have special training apart from practising the basic skills. For example, to increase the power of the legs, you can practise squat with one leg, full squat with a load, or static half squat with a load (being static for a few seconds to a few minutes). To increase the high speed power (explosive force), you can practise quick stand up after full squat with a load, continuous jumping with both feet, upward jumping with bent legs, jumping with separate legs, and jumping with alternate legs to a certain height. To increase speed, you can practise 30-metre and 60-metre runs at different speeds. You can also place your legs on wall bars to strengthen the abdominal muscles and the front muscles of the thighs, as well as increasing the ability of leg control. In short, there are many methods, and you can choose from among them for different purposes.

4. Perseverance

A proverb says: "Practise boxing one thousand times, and you acquire all skills." To practise boxing with high proficiency, you must persist in the practice hundreds of times, seriously and arduously. In other words, you must have an accumulation of "quantity" in the practice before you can achieve good coordination with hands, eyes and feet. Get to know the expressions, rhythms and rules, and the level of *Chang Quan* play will be raised quickly. Beginners are advised to practise every day. The length of time needed for practice depends on your own conditions.

In short, as long as you study accurately and diligently, you can correctly grasp the essentials and learn *Chang Quan* well.

Appendix
State Competition Regulations for Optional Long-Style Boxing Routines

In the modern long-style boxing *(Chang Quan)* competition, many Wushu trainers and competitors have introduced some new routines on the basis of their own experiences combined with the traditional Wushu theories and techniques called "optional routines." In order to encourage different styles and preserve the traditional unity, the Chinese State Physical Culture and Sports Commission has issued regulations for the optional routines in the *Chang Quan* competition. I have included the following appendix as a reference for my readers.

Regulations for Chang Quan *Competition Optional Routines*

The *Chang Quan* routines include at least the following:

1. The three hand forms—fist, palm and hook—and the five stances—bow step, horse-riding step, empty step, crouch step and seated step (no horse-riding step for women competitors). Bow step, not less than four times, and horse-riding and empty steps, not less than twice.

2. Five fist techniques (punch, not less than five times), five palm techniques and two elbow techniques (including one attacking elbow technique).

3. Leg techniques—extension and flexion, straight swing, sweep and turn, and slap (not less than two extension and flexion techniques and three times).

Only one split, and one time is permitted in the whole routine—or no splits.

4. Three different groups of balances, each static for two or more seconds.

5. Three different groups of jumping

1) Each jumping movement and each jump with hand and leg techniques are not permitted to appear more than twice, and the butterfly not more than once.

2) Run-up jumping movements are not permitted to appear more than twice in the whole routine.

6. Two tumbling movements are permitted, but twice only. One restricted movement is permitted only once. It's advisable not to include these movements.

Jumping kicks, horizontal fall with back-bend, kneeling slide, chest slide and back-turn with tucked body are not permitted.

图书在版编目（CIP）数据

长拳拳术入门：英文/程慧琨著.

－北京：外文出版社，1995

（中国武术丛书）

ISBN 7-119-01538-9

Ⅰ.长…Ⅱ.程… Ⅲ.长拳－基本知识－英文

Ⅳ. G852.12

中国版本图书馆 CIP 数据核字（1995）第 9628 号

责任编辑　　贾先锋
封面设计　　席恒青
印刷监制　　冯　浩

外文出版社网址:
　http://www.flp.com.cn
外文出版社电子信箱:
　info@flp.com.cn
　sales@flp.com.cn

长拳拳术入门
程慧琨著
★

©外文出版社

外文出版社出版

（中国北京百万庄大街 24 号）

邮政编码　100037

北京外文印刷厂印刷

中国国际图书贸易总公司发行

（中国北京车公庄西路 35 号）

北京邮政信箱第 399 号　邮政编码　100044

（大 32 开）

2003 年第 1 版第 2 次印刷

（英）

ISBN 7-119-01538-9/G·84(外)

01550

7-E-2951P